Meditations for Ministers

Mark G. Boyer

ACTA
PUBLICATIONS

Meditations for Ministers
by Mark G. Boyer

Edited by Patrice J. Tuohy and Gregory F. Augustine Pierce

Cover design by Tom A. Wright

Typesetting by Garrison Publications

Scripture quotations are from the *New Revised Standard Version of the Bible: Catholic Edition* copyright ©1993 and 1989 by the Division of Christian Education of the National Council of the Churches of Christ in the U.S.A. Used with permission. All rights reserved.

Published by: ACTA Publications
4848 North Clark Street
Chicago, IL 60640
800-397-2282
ACTApublications@aol.com

Library of Congress Catalog Number: 00-101209

ISBN: 0-87946-213-2

Printed in the United States of America

Year: 07 06 05 04 03 02 01 00

Printing: 10 9 8 7 6 5 4 3 2 1 First Printing

Contents

Dedicated to my "sister,"
Rosalie Digenan, D.C.,
friend, co-worker, confidant, supporter, minister,
50 years as a Daughter of Charity.

Introduction

Christian ministers come in all shapes, sizes, ages, genders, ethnic backgrounds, even denominational affiliations. We have a wide range of education, experience, talent, and responsibility. We are liberal, conservative, middle-of-the-road, high church, low church, introverted, extroverted, and converted. Some of us are paid (often not too well) and many of us are volunteers. The one thing we share, however, is ministry.

The dictionary defines the word *ministry* as "to give service, care, or aid; to attend, as to wants or necessities." In that sense, all Christians (and all people of good will, for that matter) are ministers. But for some of us, ministry is a conscious choice—a vocation, if you will—that forms an important part of our Christian identity and life's work, a key to our understanding of the ultimate meaning of life and our relationship with God through Jesus.

This book of reflections is specifically for ministers. We try to do so much for others that sometimes we do not take a few minutes for ourselves to reflect on what we are doing and why we are doing it. I have been a priest for almost 25 years, and I continue to struggle with the spirituality of the various ministries in which I am engaged. So I have written these meditations as much for myself as for others.

These more than 300 meditations are organized into 19 chapters around topics that are central to the Christian life: grace and sin, the sacraments, images of church, prayer, and various aspects of God and daily life. Follow them sequentially, jump around based on theme or title or scripture selection, or better yet, let the Spirit move you.

Meditations for Ministers is designed for Christian ministers of all denominations—both lay and ordained, male and female, professional and volunteer. While it is written from my own Roman Catholic perspective, I have attempted to offer some universal concepts underlying Christian ministry as we enter the third millennium of the Christian movement.

Each chapter presents a brief introduction to the primary theme, which is then fleshed out in a series of short reflections illuminated by a carefully chosen scripture passage. The idea is to read each meditation slowly and thoughtfully, perhaps one a day or several on a particular day. If you keep a journal, you may want to record your reactions and insights for future reference. Your reading and reflection may also lead you to prayer or Bible study. Perhaps these practices may even lead to a new spiritual discipline that can enrich your ministry.

However you use this book, I hope that it provides both challenge and support to your work as a minister of Christ. Thank you for your ministry. May God continue to bless it.

CHAPTER 1

Journey

People are always on the move, no matter whether we're going to work or coming home, driving to the grocery store or picking up clothes from the dry cleaner, eating dinner at a restaurant or attending a movie at the local multiplex. Each journey begins with the first step, and each journey can be the means through which God reveals a little more of the divine reality to us. Journey, or pilgrimage, is a theme of rich fare for God's people. The wandering Hebrews became the Israelites exiled from Jerusalem and, then, the Jews who returned to the holy city. Jesus was an itinerant preacher who had "nowhere to lay his head" (Luke 9:58). As Christian ministers, we do well to imitate the Master and begin with reflections on our own journey—where we have been and where we are going. As we stand in the middle of it, we can be assured that God will guide our steps.

Renewal

❦ A journey, no matter when you decide to begin it, offers you the opportunity to be renewed, refreshed, and refocused. "Do not be conformed to this world," Paul tells the Romans, "but be transformed by the renewing of your minds, so that you may discern what is the will of God—what is good and acceptable and perfect" (Romans 12:2). Make a point right now to raise your awareness of how you conform to cultural expectations—your style of dress, the type of music you listen to, your work ethic, etc.—and consider how you can discern God's will for you by making changes that will transform your life. The result of your work will be renewal.

> **WISDOM 18:3** *You provided a flaming pillar of fire as a guide for your people's unknown journey, and a harmless sun for their glorious wandering.*

Passing through

❦ Most people take themselves too seriously, and Christian ministers are particularly susceptible to this. Our vision of the future seems to us to be limitless, when in fact it is very limited. We are on a pilgrimage that may last somewhere between 70 and 100 years—maybe a few less, maybe a few more. All that we think is important right now fades to insignificance when we begin to think about how short our lives are. We're just passing through; we're not here to stay forever. If we keep that thought in mind, we won't take ourselves so seriously and might, paradoxically, live our lives more deeply.

> **MARK 6:8-9** *[Jesus] ordered [his disciples] to take nothing for their journey except a staff; no bread, no bag, no money in their belts; but to wear sandals and not to put on two tunics.*

Linear time

❦ Most people create a mental image of their life's journey as linear. They draw a time line on a sheet of paper and, beginning with the day of birth, mark the major events of their lives on the line. The line indicates that their lives are going somewhere into the future. And that may be true for some years, but it's not true forever. Just as there is a beginning to your time line (birth), there is also an end (death). The author of Ecclesiastes says, "There is a time for every matter under heaven: a time to be born, and a time to die" (3:1-2). What's important is what you do on your pilgrimage in between the beginning and the end.

> **TOBIT 10:11** *[Raguel told Tobias,] "Farewell, my child; have a safe journey. The LORD of heaven prosper you and your wife Sarah, and may I see children of yours before I die."*

A time to be born

❦ People tend to think of birth as a one-time event. In a definite year, on a specific day, within one of 24 hours, at a certain minute, you were born; you have a birth certificate to prove it. You emerged from your mother's womb and took your first breath. There is a "time to be born" (Ecclesiastes 3:2). But there is also a time to be reborn, a time, according to Saint Paul, to "walk in newness of life" (Romans 6:4). Your rebirth occurred the day you were baptized, but it has been repeated every time you decided to change your life. It's the ongoing rebirths that make your life worth living and makes it a model for others as a Christian minister.

> **TITUS 3:5** *[God] saved us, not because of any works of righteousness that we had done, but according to his mercy, through the water of rebirth and renewal by the Holy Spirit.*

A time to die

❦ When Ecclesiastes says there is "a time to die" (3:2), we may feel shock at first—since who thinks about death? Then we might experience depression—since who wants to leave the people, home, and goods we've worked so hard to get? Unlike the opportunity for daily rebirth, we don't get to "practice" death. Paul tells the Romans "that all of us who were baptized into Christ Jesus were baptized into his death" (Romans 6:3). That death with Christ should prepare us for our "time to die." Once we accept the inevitability of our death, we are prepared to really live. Death gives life meaning. By knowing our end, we are able to make better use of our present time, which is a good example to give as a Christian minister.

> **1 JOHN 3:14** *We know that we have passed from death to life because we love one another. Whoever does not love abides in death.*

Pack light

❦ As we pilgrimage from birth to death, most of us gather people and things. We may have a spouse, children, and all types of in-laws and friends. We have houses, cars, pictures, dishes, tools, etc. While people and things can assist us on our journey, they can also become a burden that we have to carry. "Pack light" is a slogan that should be every pilgrim's guide. It lessens our need to be concerned with what we've brought along and it enables us to focus our attention on what really matters—living. You're a smart minister if you have frequent garage sales to eliminate the clutter in your life.

> **LUKE 9:3** *[Jesus said to the twelve,] "Take nothing for your journey, no staff, nor bag, nor bread, no money—not even an extra tunic."*

Destination

❦ When you take a trip, you usually have a destination in mind. You might be going to the grocery store or you may be taking a vacation across the country, but you know where you're headed. What's true of your daily life is also true of a lifetime. As a Christian minister, you need to have a long-range plan, a vision, of where you're headed. God told Abraham, "Go from your country and your kindred and your father's house to the land that I will show you" (Genesis 12:1). Abraham trusted that God knew the destination. Jesus has already revealed our destination—God's house (see John 14:1-7). Knowing your destination enables you to recognize and avoid detours whenever possible.

> **MARK 13:34** *"It is like a man going on a journey, when he leaves home and puts his slaves in charge, each with his work, and commands the doorkeeper to be on the watch."*

Fear of the unknown

❦ While excitement often permeates our life's journey, making a change in plans can produce fear. We are afraid of what we don't know or what we have yet to experience. Abraham and Sarah must have known this type of fear. They "set out not knowing where [they were] going" (Hebrews 11:8). We're not like that old couple, however. We've been shown the way by Jesus. God's words, spoken by the prophet Isaiah, offer us comfort: "Do not fear, for I have redeemed you; I have called you by name, you are mine" (Isaiah 43:1). Thus can we travel without fear of the unknown. God says, "Do not fear, for I am with you" (Isaiah 43:5). That ought to be a message every Christian minister proclaims.

> **TOBIT 5:22** *[Tobit said,] "A good angel will accompany [Tobias]; his journey will be successful, and he will come back in good health."*

First step

✤ No matter at what time in your life you find yourself ready to begin your pilgrimage of change again, you only need to take the hardest step—the first one. It's easy to find reasons to procrastinate or become momentarily distracted. But with a little effort, you can get started. Once you do, you will regain the enthusiasm you experienced earlier in your life. It's no accident that *enthusiasm* literally means "filled with God." God will strengthen you and get you back on track, usually without your awareness of the divine presence leading the way.

> **WISDOM 19:4-5** *The fate they deserved drew them on . . . and made them forget what had happened, in order . . . that your people might experience an incredible journey.*

CHAPTER 2

Grace

G race is like a river; it flows from God to us and continues through us to others—until it brings everyone back to its source. As Christian ministers, we can recognize grace both in our own lives and in the lives of those to whom we minister. While we can't open our hands and have a cupful of grace poured into them, by reflecting on our lives we can know that God has been at work in them. And by helping others reflect on their lives, we can help people begin to see the ways that God has traced grace through their own experiences. Ministry is fired over and over again when grace meets grace and it is recognized.

Beyond yourself

❧ Being human means being able to experience transcendence, going beyond yourself and realizing that you share divine life with all of creation. In other words, being human somehow implies also being divine. This ability to experience existence as transcendence can come from no where other than the Creator. Through your transcendent experiences, you get glimpses of your divinity as you seek to become all that you can be, a process that lasts a lifetime.

> **2 PETER 3:18** *Grow in the grace and knowledge of our Lord and Savior Jesus Christ. To him be the glory both now and to the day of eternity. Amen.*

God in our midst

❧ Another way to talk about the divine life human beings share is to call it grace. Grace is God's never-ending communication with us. No matter what skin color, what gender, what height, we all share graceful existence with one another and with God. Grace suddenly erupts in our experiences of ministering to people, and we find ourselves in the presence of God.

> **1 PETER 4:10** *Like good stewards of the manifold grace of God, serve one another with whatever gift each of you has received.*

To know fully

❧ Your self-awareness is what makes you a spiritual being. This transcendental character of your existence, this experience of self, is also and simultaneously the experience of God. Any common human experience, because it is grounded in God, can be the beginning point for probing your life to see how God has been at work in you. Yet being self-aware and continuing to become more self-aware is a lifetime process. Saint Paul writes that we can "know only in part . . . but when the complete comes, the partial will come to an end. Now I know only in part; then I will know fully, even as I have been fully known" (1 Corinthians 13:12-13).

> **1 Peter 1:13** *Prepare your minds for action; discipline yourselves; set all your hope on the grace that Jesus Christ will bring you when he is revealed.*

What freedom brings

❦ Through self-awareness, you realize that you are a free and responsible being, yet one who is dependent upon history for help in your quest for self-knowledge. What little you can know of the divine, you have learned by observing God at work in the world, specifically in your own life. This is an important gift that you bring to your ministry. You are wed to the world—to matter and to history—and it is in the world that you discover God. In other words, you experience yourself as existing both within and beyond limits, with questions that end in mystery.

> **1 Peter 1:10** *Concerning this salvation, the prophets who prophesied of the grace that was to be yours made careful search and inquiry.*

In God's image

❦ Our desire to know is infinite, always exceeding our grasp of the known. By focusing our desire to know on our relationships, we come to know both other people and God intimately. Each person flashes forth some aspect of the divine presence—the "image of God"—a spark of God's life that orients us toward union with God.

If we try, all of us can aspire to taste and see the divine, to whom we are inevitably drawn as our final end. All of us have a capacity for the infinite and absolute.

> **GENESIS 1:27** *God created humankind in his image, in the image of God he created them; male and female he created them.*

Comparable relationships

❧ Beginning with our experience of intimate human relationships, we can discover a paradigm, a habit of thinking, for our relationship with God. However, we must also be aware that, whatever we say about divine-human relationships, using the human-relationship metaphor is only a feeble beginning in our attempt to understand the undefinable God. As human beings, we must acknowledge that only God loves perfectly. Furthermore, through our human relationships, we do not make God present, as if we can control God. Rather, God is always present in and through human relationships, but we are not always aware of this divine gift.

> **1 JOHN 4:16** *God is love, and those who abide in love abide in God, and God abides in them.*

Invitation

❧ Initiating a relationship with another usually begins with extreme caution, as self-consciousness seems to prohibit us from sharing more than what is peripheral to our humanity. Only our accidentals are revealed, such as hair color, place of birth, interests, accomplishments. The same is true when another initiates a relationship with us. He or she begins with what is accidental to his or her humanity. Even though we know that God is seeking expression through human relationships, we are reticent to openness. Sooner or later, however, both parties must recognize that their self-descriptions, while useful in distinguishing one person from another, are but means to an end: God's revelation.

1 John 4:12 *No one has ever seen God; if we love one another, God lives in us, and his love is perfected in us.*

The dance begins

Once the first move is made and another person accepts your invitation to relationship, you both begin to enter into deeper levels of sharing. This does not come automatically or immediately, but very cautiously. The degree that one of you reveals your humanity corresponds to the degree that the other does the same. This is ministry in action. Together you form a dialectic and then a process of reconciling your differences. Depending upon the two persons involved in a relationship, this movement can continue over days, months, or years.

1 John 4:8 *Whoever does not love does not know God, for God is love.*

Intimacy encountered

Each time you encounter another, you move quickly through the various levels of humanity you have already probed together and, gradually, achieve intimacy, that state where you are totally you and the other is totally he or she. In essence, you stand naked before the other, as there is increasingly little that you do not share. The relationship continues to delve into intimacy as long as both parties continue to support and, simultaneously, challenge each other. It is at this point that you become aware that you are both grace—a sign of God's presence—for the other.

1 JOHN 4:7 *Beloved, let us love one another, because love is from God; everyone who loves is born of God and knows God.*

More and less

❧ Intimacy between two people involves the dialectic of enrichment and diminishment. Enrichment comes from what is shared. You are enriched by another person in a relationship by the clarifications the other person helps you make about yourself, particularly through his or her challenge that you are not being honest with yourself or with others. Yet you are diminished even as you are enriched, because you must die to yourself to find yourself. Diminishment comes as you give up some of your ego to help the other person achieve identity and honesty with himself or herself.

> **2 THESSALONIANS 1:3** *We must give thanks to God for you, brothers and sisters, as is right, because your faith is growing abundantly, and the love of everyone of you for one another is increasing.*

Surges of energy

❧ The simultaneous enrichment and diminishment experienced through intimacy with another is often referred to as "chemistry" between two people. There is excitement and anxiety, love and conflict, in the freedom both people enjoy in a relationship. Their freedom is an energy that passes between them, like electricity between two cars hooked up with battery cables. Both are simultaneously jump-started and drained.

> **1 CORINTHIANS 2:9** *As it is written, "What no eye has seen, nor ear heard, nor the human heart conceived, what God has prepared for those who love him."*

The story unfolds

The deepest of mysteries is the story of your relationships with others and with God. Through your relationships you move outside of yourself and experience transcendence. The narrative of your life unfolds and keeps growing and improving as long as you choose to relate to others and share in God's grace with others.

> **HEBREWS 4:16** *Let us . . . approach the throne of grace with boldness, so that we may receive mercy and find grace to help in time of need.*

We are who we are

Saint Paul says, "By the grace of God I am what I am and his grace toward me has not been in vain" (1 Corinthians 15:10). Not only are we who we are, but because of grace experienced through relationships, we are always in the process of becoming who we are meant to be. Ministry is a process. From our youthful introduction to intimate friendship we become aware that the energy and love we share with friends is nothing other than God's Spirit, or grace. Once we've experienced love, we want more of it. And that desire continues. It is expressed through our ministry.

> **TITUS 2:11** *The grace of God has appeared, bringing salvation to all.*

Free to be

Possessiveness is not a part of intimacy. Without thoughtful reflection, human beings have an inclination to cling to the person who offers them love, affection, friendship, care, or support. But relationships must be entered into freely and both parties must remain free. Indeed, such freedom is the ground for making a relationship even possible. Freedom is the ground for all ministry. Possessiveness removes the basis for a relationship to grow, for grace to be shared. Possessiveness smothers the fire of a relationship.

> **2 TIMOTHY 1:9** *[God] saved us and called us with a holy calling, not according to our works but according to his own purpose and grace. This grace was given to us in Christ Jesus before the ages began.*

Under these conditions

✿ In relationships, we can easily confuse unconditional love with unconditional approval. God loves us unconditionally. There are no conditions that we must meet to earn God's love. But God does not always approve of our behavior—just as we don't always approve of our beloved's behavior or he or she of ours. But like God's unconditional love for us, we don't give up loving one another. As hurts heal, we begin relating and growing again—forgiven and forgiving.

> **ROMANS 5:1-2** *We have peace with God through our Lord Jesus Christ, through whom we have obtained access to this grace in which we stand.*

Our defenses are down

✿ Intimacy makes us vulnerable. We can hurt one another easily because we know the other's weaknesses. As we share those inner dimensions of ourselves and receive the grace from another who is doing the same, we bring each other to a state of openness. We no longer protect ourselves because the other has assisted in creating an environment of love. This is how we are prepared for a relationship with God. Offering us grace, God moves us to respond. We are vulnerable, because God knows us better than we know ourselves, but we trust in God's love for us. This vulnerability and trust is essential in all relationships and all true ministries.

> **ACTS 20:22** *[Paul said,] "Now, as a captive to the Spirit, I am on my way to Jerusalem, not knowing what will happen to me there."*

Ready or not

❦ There are occasions in our lives when our encounters with others are entered into quickly and only for a short time. The encounter may take place after church on Sunday, after class in college, or in a chance encounter with another person during a convention or meeting. These moments of instant intimacy remind us that God breaks into our lives on God's time—not ours—and prepares us— through others—to receive God.

> **ROMANS 1:7** *To all God's beloved in Rome, who are called to be saints: Grace to you and peace from God our Father and the LORD Jesus Christ.*

Love: a work in process

❦ Your relationship with God continues an infinite process. As you become more of who you are, you recognize more of who God is. In a sense, God "becomes" more real by virtue of this ongoing relationship with you.

> **ROMANS 12:3** *For by the grace given to me I say to everyone among you not to think of yourself more highly than you ought to think, but to think with sober judgment, each according to the measure of faith that God has assigned.*

The more you know

❦ You come to know who you are through relating with others, and your relationships become more authentic as you come to know yourself better. Through your intimate personal relationships, you experience transcendence and see yourself as a whole person, designed by God to be more than who you experience yourself to be on your own.

> **COLOSSIANS 3:9-10** *You have stripped off the old self with its practices and have clothed yourselves with the new self, which is being renewed in knowledge according to the image of its creator.*

Tools of self-knowledge

❦ To come to a deeper knowledge of yourself, you can use psychological tools of measurement. For example, if you are careful not to let others define you and, thus, lose your independent and unique identity, the use of personality type indicators can help you know yourself. In the process of knowing yourself, you free yourself from self-consciousness and become comfortable being yourself in the world. This freedom enables you to minister better to others. It enables you to free them to be who they are and to relate to you if they so desire. Freedom enables you to recognize that every person has the potential for manifesting the presence of God.

> **2 PETER 1:5-7** *You must make every effort to support your faith with goodness, and goodness with knowledge, and knowledge with self-control, and self-control with endurance, and endurance with godliness, and godliness with mutual affection, and mutual affection with love.*

At your core

❦ Through self-reflection, you will come to realize that as a spiritual being you possess an inherent orientation toward God. At your core you desire a relationship with God, who waits for you in your silence and aloneness, like a patient lover waiting for his or her beloved. As love deepens, lovers delve deeper and deeper into the mystery of each other. So it will be with you and God, who exists at the core of every person's existence.

> **PSALMS 31:14** *I trust in you, O LORD; I say, "You are my God."*

Contact with God

❦ By knowing ourselves, we make contact with God. By touching others and permitting them to touch us, we experience divine presence. By reflecting on our human ways of relating, we understand how God relates to us individually—and collectively. Ministry is merely helping others relate to God in the same way we have learned to do.

> **PSALMS 59:17** *O my strength, I will sing praises to you, for you, O God, are my fortress, the God who shows me steadfast love.*

Created in love

❦ Just as we offer one another the invitation to enter into relationships, God does the same. God initiates relationships with human beings. In some sense, it is true to say that each of us is already connected to God by the very fact of our being. God first creates a creature who is loveable and then offers divine love to that person.

PSALMS 63:1 *O God, you are my God, I seek you, my soul thirsts for you; my flesh faints for you, as in a dry and weary land where there is no water.*

God's offer

❦ Human freedom is a prerequisite for any relationship. You cannot relate to another in fear, nor can you relate to another who thrusts a relationship upon you. This is also true of your relationship with God. Just as in human relationships, where the initiator waits to see if he or she gets any response to an initial move, so, too, does God wait for a response from you. You have the freedom to accept or reject God's offer. If you accept, you open yourself to the divine mystery.

> **EPHESIANS 3:5** *In former generations this mystery was not made known to humankind, as it has now been revealed to [the] holy apostles and prophets by the Spirit.*

Graceful activity

❦ Grace is the act of relationship between one person and another in intimacy grounded in mutual love and respect. Grace is also the act of relationship between God and us. Our experience of this relationship causes us to continue to act until we have achieved total union with the one in whom we "live and move and have [our] being" (Acts 17:28).

> **PHILIPPIANS 2:5-7** *Christ Jesus, who, though he was in the form of God, did not regard equality with God as something to be exploited, . . . emptied himself, taking the form of a slave, being born in human likeness.*

The offer stands

✤ Just as you are making offers to others to enter into personal relationships throughout your life, so God makes the offer of grace throughout the whole of your life. And just as you can never be 100 percent sure where you are in relationship to another person, you can never be sure exactly where you are with God's offer of relationship to you, although the offer is always there and always demanding some response. As in any relationship, the degree or intensity of your relationship with God will differ from time to time.

> **HEBREWS 12:1** *Since we are surrounded by so great a cloud of witnesses, let us also lay aside every weight and . . . run with perseverance the race that is set before us.*

Abundance

✤ Responding to God's offer of grace, we suddenly discover that even more has been given to us as a result of our response. We are further freed to continue the discovery of who we are, a process that lasts a lifetime—and maybe even beyond. Christian ministers facilitate this process for others until those to whom we minister are able to recognize God's abundant grace in their lives.

> **2 PETER 1:2** *May grace and peace be yours in abundance in the knowledge of God and of Jesus our Lord.*

Waiting to be filled

✤ Two people in a loving relationship free each other to be totally who they are and to revel in their freedom. They experience growing together as a simultaneous growing apart (as they come to know who they are and who they are not as individuals). They mold each other in freedom, just as God molds each of us, until we are capable of being filled with divine life.

WISDOM 15:7 *A potter kneads the soft earth and labori-ously molds each vessel for our service.*

CHAPTER 3

Sin

Even though we experience ourselves surrounded by grace, as limited human beings we also know when we haven't been all that God has called us to be. We name this state of existence *sin*. As ministers, we know that we often don't live up to our potential. That experience enables us to help others. Instead of condemning the failures of others, we respect their humanity. In that exchange of understanding, grace overwhelms sin, and others leave our presence with the forgiveness that flows from God to and through us.

Balancing act

🌿 What we experience as human beings is that we simultaneously share and do not share in God's life. We are becoming who we are meant to be, and we are failing to become who we are meant to be. We are free, and we are not free. In the tension between being and not being, becoming and not becoming, freedom and slavery, we experience life. Like a rubber band stretched between two poles, we discover that real living is found exactly where we didn't want to look—in the tension itself. And we also discover that when we are really living we are achieving wholeness, a balance in the tension.

> **ROMANS 8:3** *God has done what the law, weakened by the flesh, could not do: by sending his own Son in the likeness of sinful flesh, and to deal with sin, he condemned sin in the flesh.*

The choice is ours

🌿 Ministers do not always choose grace. In human relationships, we may hurt the other through what we say or don't say, through what action we do or don't take. In our relationship with God, we have similar choices and limitations. In other words, we have the ability to sin. As we can with other people, we can also reject God, although in doing so we are also rejecting the only one who can make us whole.

> **ROMANS 5:16** *The free gift is not like the effect of the one man's sin. For the judgment following one trespass brought condemnation, but the free gift following many trespasses brings justification.*

Original options

❦ The experience of being stretched away from wholeness—away from God—is called original sin. We encounter this experience daily. It is our ability not to notice the person in need, not to hear another's problems, not to minister when asked. However, original sin cannot compare to the power of original grace. When the two tug at each other, grace overwhelms sin and brings us closer to the wholeness of God.

> **ROMANS 5:21** *Just as sin exercised dominion in death, so grace might also exercise dominion through justification leading to eternal life through Jesus Christ our Lord.*

Worst enemy

❦ Human beings have a tendency to become our own worst enemies. We have the ability to experience transcendence—being more than who we are—at the same time that we experience a capacity to be less than who we are. Be assured that grace is more powerful than sin, however. Humans are free to choose either good or evil, but we are called toward the good.

> **JAMES 4:17** *Anyone . . . who knows the right thing to do and fails to do it, commits sin.*

Deny God, deny self

❦ When we do not accept God's repeated offer of a relationship, we are, in effect, denying who we are and who we are called to be. Only God can make us whole, totally alive. Without grace, without relationships, we choose to be slaves to ourselves and our possessions. We take without giving. The result is alienation and ultimately despair.

Romans 8:3 *The law of the Spirit of life in Christ Jesus has set you free from the law of sin and of death.*

Be your true self

❦ What you do with your freedom in a relationship depends on who you are and who you are becoming. Sin represents being who you are not called to be. You withdraw from your true self and fail to accept responsibility for your own life. As you minister, sin means also failing to help others immerse themselves in their own humanity and take responsibility for their lives.

> **Romans 7:20** *Now if I do what I do not want, it is no longer I that do it, but sin that dwells within me.*

The wages of sin

❦ Sin is the failure to respond to God by deciding that you can become who you are meant to be without the help of others. And while God doesn't stop anyone from going it alone, the solitary road is not very productive. Security and safety are found in relationships with others. That security is not a warm, cozy feeling but the freedom to probe the mystery of the other, which puts you in contact with the divinity you are becoming. God became human in Jesus so that everyone can become divine in one another.

> **Romans 6:23** *The wages of sin is death, but the free gift of God is eternal life in Christ Jesus our Lord.*

See the total picture

❦ Sometimes people get so overwhelmed by evil that they think they can do nothing by themselves. But sin is never the total picture.

Ministers don't begin with sin and then get to grace. We begin with grace, which is more powerful, and then notice the sin. Our lives are graced horizons toward which we are always on pilgrimage, always in process. We can never be totally out of grace, because God loves us and offers us grace, even when we are not ready to accept it.

> **ROMANS 6:22** *Now that you have been freed from sin and enslaved to God, the advantage you get is sanctification. The end is eternal life.*

CHAPTER 4

Jesus Christ

The model of Christian ministry is Jesus Christ. He gave form to ministry by calling tax collectors, adulterers, sinners, and other societal outcasts and eating with them. He associated himself with lepers, healed the sick, and proclaimed that God's reign was in their midst. God was present, said Jesus, exactly where they weren't looking—in themselves, the least members of society. Jesus didn't begin a corporation and then start a department called "Ministry." He began to serve the needs of people by telling them that God was already with them. The way Jesus practiced ministry was unlimited and unstructured and uncontrolled. While we Christian ministers today usually represent a specific church, we do well to remember that ministry is to all God's people.

Model for relationship

❦ Jesus modeled the relationship between God and humans. He called God "Abba," a familiar term for "Father" that indicated the intimacy between them. What set Jesus apart was his complete faithfulness to that relationship. While we often stumble and fall, hurting the ones we love, Jesus never did. He remained faithful to God unto his death. Jesus did what God intended for all people: he became totally human. And he did what all people are intended to do: to receive the offer of God's grace. We Christian ministers model humanity open to grace through our service to others.

> **JOHN 1:16** *From [the Word's] fullness we have all received, grace upon grace.*

Word made flesh

❦ God became human in the person of Jesus of Nazareth. Two Christian feasts focus on this Christian mystery: the Annunciation and Christmas. The Annunciation (March 25) celebrates the conception of Jesus in Mary's womb, the beginning of his enfleshment. Christmas (December 25), often referred to as the Incarnation, recalls the day of Jesus' birth. Christians profess this belief in the Creed when they say that Jesus became human. But what is different about Jesus is that he is also God. In the words of the Creed, he is "true God from true God, begotten, not made, one in being with the Father." It is Jesus the "true God" who teaches us how to become human.

> **JOHN 1:14** *The Word became flesh and lived among us, and we have seen his glory, the glory as of a father's only son, full of grace and truth.*

Perfect person

❦ Jesus represents the culmination of God's divine plan for us. While we can never begin to understand this plan adequately, Jesus serves as the image of a perfected human being. He is the example of how grace triumphs—even through death. He kept his focus on grace and cooperated with it, even when tempted. In him, the divine is expressed by the human, and the human discloses the divine. Jesus is God with a face. Thus, what is human and what is divine have been united in one person perfectly. Sometimes we Christian ministers must awaken the divine in people, and sometimes we must awaken the human. Otherwise, we cannot guide them to wholeness.

> **John 1:17** *The law indeed was given through Moses; grace and truth came through Jesus Christ.*

The freedom of surrender

❦ The union of the human and divine in Jesus can be understood by reflecting on a relationship you share with a friend or a spouse. The intimacy between you and the other does not take away freedom or individuality but enhances the freedom of both of you and fosters each person's uniqueness. Likewise, Jesus demonstrated that his wholeness is the wholeness God desires for everyone. The divine and the human are not in opposition. It is through your surrender to another that freedom and individuality arise, just as through surrender to God Jesus' freedom and individuality arose.

> **John 1:18** *No one has ever seen God. It is God the only Son, who is close to the Father's heart, who has made him known.*

Wholeness

❧ Jesus is a paradigm for embodied wholeness. He is the proof of God's decision to share divine life with humanity. It was through the dynamic of his relationship with God that Jesus experienced wholeness. It is through the dynamic of our relationship with God that we, too, will be made whole.

> **JOHN 1:1, 14** *In the beginning was the Word, and the Word was with God, and the Word was God. And the Word became flesh and lived among us.*

Leavening agents

❧ Jesus spoke about wholeness in terms of leaven, the agent used in the ancient world to make dough rise. Leaven, however, was considered corrupt, rotten, evil. That is why the Book of Exodus makes clear that the feast of Passover, a day commemorating God's liberation of the people of Israel from slavery, must be celebrated with unleavened bread. Those who are whole have been "corrupted" by God, said Jesus. As leaven causes dough to expand, so too we, who have been touched by God, are puffed up with the Spirit. And everyone we minister to is likewise "corrupted" by God.

> **MATTHEW 13:33** *"The kingdom of heaven is like yeast that a woman took and mixed in with three measures of flour until all of it was leavened."*

Like treasure

❧ When you find a friend with whom you enter into a relationship of intimacy, that person is a treasure to you and you are a treasure to him or her. Every person to whom you minister is a treasure hidden in the field of self, culture, worry, stress. Your task is to both find and show others the treasures they contain. In so doing, you will reveal your own treasure. The wholeness you will experience is God reigning in your life.

> **MATTHEW 13:44** *"The kingdom of heaven is like treasure hidden in a field, which someone found and hid; then in his joy he goes and sells all that he has and buys that field."*

Risky investments

✤ Wholeness, as preached by Jesus, is like the purchase of a precious gem. Before you buy a diamond, ruby, or emerald, you examine it from every angle. You admire the light reflected through its facets. You calculate its cost. Then you determine whether it is worth your investment. Those who minister to the needs of others look upon others as precious gems through whom God's light—grace—shines. The cost of these gems is your willingness to share your grace with them. If you don't, they may not share any of their grace with you. It's only by taking risks that you can own precious gems.

> **MATTHEW 13:45-46** *"The kingdom of heaven is like a merchant in search of fine pearls; on finding one pearl of great value, he went and sold all that he had and bought it."*

Share your talents

✤ Christian ministers help people recognize the gifts God has given to them. The use of one's gifts is the way to wholeness. In Jesus' parable of the talents, for example, the slave who received one talent presumed that his master was a harsh person. In his fear, he hid the talent and did not risk developing it as his fellow gift-receivers did. As a result of his folly, he not only lost his gift, but he missed the opportunity for the wholeness that would have come with taking the risk to use the abilities he had. Every time you minister to another, you take a risk. But it is ultimately a step toward the wholeness that God offers each of us.

> **MATTHEW 25:26-27** *"You wicked and lazy slave! You knew, did you, that I reap where I did not sow, and gather where I did not scatter? Then you ought to have invested my money with the bankers, and on my return I would have received what was my own with interest."*

Confluence

When we love another, we offer a share in the divine stream that courses through us. When others accept our offer, they offer in return a share in the divine stream that courses through them. There is no distinction between divine love and truly human love. When we love others, we love and share in God. When others love us, they love and share in God. Thus do people become the embodiment of God's gift of self. Ministry is the act of both giving and receiving love and discovering that it is God who is shared in the loving.

> **JOHN 15:12** *"This is my commandment, that you love one another as I have loved you."*

Intimacy and freedom

When two human beings enter into a state of intimacy, they also experience the freedom to be themselves. The more intimate they become, the freer and more vulnerable they are in each other's presence. And the freer and more vulnerable they are in each other's presence, the easier they plumb the depths of intimacy. Likewise, the closer we are to God, the more freedom we experience. Jesus, incarnate grace, lived in complete intimacy and freedom with God and with others. He became the paradigm for all relationships.

JOHN 8:32 *"You will know the truth, and the truth will make you free."*

Become fully aware

Jesus is the icon of the person who fulfilled his humanity. He lived for God, and others could see that in his person. His life flowed from the divine source, upon which he relied for meaning and wholeness. Jesus' life was grounded in his growing awareness of God's presence in his life and his ever-deepening understanding of his intimate union with God. Our being aware of God's presence is essential in our ministry. While we cannot hope to reach the level of awareness Jesus achieved, he is the model for what we all seek. His life enables us to see humanity in its highest form—expressing the divine and being a vehicle for God's revelation.

JOHN 14:9 *"Whoever has seen me has seen the Father."*

Take time out

Jesus often went away to pray, to be alone, to enter into communion with God. Christian ministers must do the same. Otherwise, we will fail to detect the direct stream of grace that surrounds us at all times. Solitude enables us to see once again by the light of God.

JOHN 1:5 *The light shines in the darkness, and the darkness did not overcome it.*

Raised from the dead

❦ The crowning of Jesus' humanity through death and resurrection will be the crowning of your humanity through death and resurrection. God validated Jesus' faithfulness by raising him from the dead. That's the result of any authentic relationship—new life, as two individuals die to the self and become one with the other. Just as every act of Jesus manifested the divine, so do your acts reveal some of the myriad possibilities of who God is. God works through you and unleashes the power of death and new life through your ministry.

> **HEBREWS 2:18** *Because he himself was tested by what he suffered, he is able to help those who are being tested.*

Find yourself in God

❦ Jesus possessed the unique relationship of divine Son to divine Father, and that is what makes him unique, gives him his identity, and makes him a paradigm for Christian ministers. Every person has the potential for manifesting the presence of the divine. God shines through more brightly every time death to self occurs. Jesus not only reminds us of this, but he is the incarnation of this.

> **JOHN 8:12** *"I am the light of the world. Whoever follows me will never walk in darkness but will have the light of life."*

Facing God

❦ Jesus shows us the face of God. But Jesus also makes us aware that all human faces express God. Every human being has a spark of the divine. As we Christian ministers reveal the presence of God in our own lives to others, we become aware that others reveal the presence of God in their lives, as well. Thus, in a sense, God meets God through a human encounter. Or in other words, every human being is an exposition of the face of God.

> **JOHN 3:31** *The one who comes from above is above all; the one who is of the earth belongs to the earth and speaks about earthly things. The one who comes from heaven is above all.*

Bearers of the Spirit

❦ As a teacher like Jesus, you enter into a relationship with your students. You set up the atmosphere of trust which frees them to study, discuss issues openly, share their opinions and perspectives without fear of ridicule. That makes the classroom a place of self-discovery for both the students and you. You share in one another's humanity. You and your students become bearers of the Spirit of Jesus.

> **JOHN 3:2** *[Nicodemus said,] "Rabbi, we know that you are a teacher who has come from God; for no one can do these signs that you do apart from the presence of God."*

Open to learning

❦ Just as God loves each of us as we are, so those of us who are teachers learn to love our students as they are and not as we wish them to be. As that begins to happen, they begin to accept us as we really are. That exchange acknowledges that each of us brings God to the other, that each of us is simultaneously teacher and learner. That's how Jesus approached the people to whom he ministered.

> **JOHN 3:10** *Jesus answered [Nicodemus], "Are you a teacher of Israel, and yet you do not understand these things?"*

We don't deserve it

❦ Nothing we can do will ever put us in a position to say that we deserve the gift of grace. If it could be earned, then it would no longer be a gift, wholly ours to embrace. If that were the case, then God could randomly pick to whom grace would be given in a capricious and fickle manner. But that is not the case. Through Jesus, the intimate life of the triune God has been shared totally with us—and we did nothing to deserve it.

> **ROMANS 5:1-2** *Since we are justified by faith, we have peace with God through our Lord Jesus Christ, through whom we have obtained access to this grace in which we stand.*

Share your good fortune

❦ The gospels portray Jesus as a healer, a mediator of the Spirit. But there was always a social response to his miracles. For example, in the Gospel of Mark, Jesus healed Simon's mother-in-law, who got out of bed so that she could serve some of his followers; a leper, who began to spread the good news everywhere; and a paralytic, who responded by glorifying God to everyone he could find. More and more, ministers see the need for a community sharing of the physical blessing of health. The Holy Spirit moves both ministers and those who are healed to somehow share the gift of grace both have received.

> **MARK 1:34** *[Jesus] cured many who were sick with various diseases.*

Put people first

❧ We ministers can become so focused on our ministry that we don't see the people who are the object of our ministry. Jesus always put people first. In Mark's Gospel, when he healed a man with a withered hand, he put the welfare of the man ahead of the Sabbath prohibition against work. Legalists, observing Jesus' action, were outraged by his obvious disregard for the law. But Jesus restored more than a withered extremity; he restored people to the first place of ministry and revealed that God is interested in people and their problems. When the law caused a human being to wither, Jesus took the necessary steps to promote healing, including freeing the person from the law. That's what it means to minister.

> **MARK 3:5** *[Jesus] said to the man, "Stretch out your hand." He stretched it out, and his hand was restored.*

Personal touch

❧ Society has a way of dividing people between the "insiders" and the "outsiders." In the ancient world, leprosy (really any type of skin disease) made one an outcast. Lepers were feared—not just because one might contract their disease, but because by touching a leper one became socially and religiously unclean. Jesus ignored all these fears and ministered to lepers by touching them. When he did so, he aligned himself with those who were on the outside. We Christian ministers must always be aware that our ministry is first and foremost to the outcasts and marginalized.

> **MARK 1:40** *[A leper said to Jesus,] "If you choose, you can make me clean."*

Equal treatment

❦ Instead of focusing on a disability, ministers must focus on the person. Jesus demonstrated this in his ministry. He treated each person equally, no matter what disability he or she had. Before God, all people are of equal human dignity. Seeing people instead of problems enables us to minister to those people who are challenged to live in a world designed by others.

> **MARK 2:11** *[Jesus said to the paralytic,] "I say to you, stand up, take you mat and go to your home."*

Indirect cures

❦ When we Christian ministers serve others, we often touch the lives of people who are not intended to be the recipients of our ministry. While counseling a grieving spouse, for example, we may give comfort to other members of the family. Such is the story about Jesus restoring life to a 12-year-old girl. The direct object of Jesus' ministry was the girl, but those who reaped the harvest of Jesus' words were many. Faith is often awakened in those who stand on the periphery of ministry.

> **MARK 5:42** *Immediately the girl got up and began to walk about (she was 12 years of age). At this they were overcome with amazement.*

Power-filled lives

❦ Lazarus' two sisters, Martha and Mary, were led to deeper levels of faith and life because of Jesus' ministry to them after their brother's death. In serving them, Jesus not only called forth Lazarus from the tomb but also called the two sisters to a faith that is meant to be a model for Christian ministers today. Jesus made it clear that he wanted them to believe in his life-giving powers, in his mastery over death.

> **JOHN 11:25-26** *Jesus said to [Martha], "I am the resurrection and the life. Those who believe in me, even though they die, will live, and everyone who lives and believes in me will never die. Do you believe this?"*

Are you hungry?

Before we can minister to another, we must be able to accept ministry from others. Such was Jesus' ministry. His act of multiplying loaves and fishes, for example, might have been achieved by a miraculous ability to get people to share what little each had. Once the sharing began, it could not be stopped. It overflowed, resulting in twelve baskets of leftovers. Jesus' hungry followers were taught to feed others, even as they were fed by others.

> **MARK 6:42** *All ate and were filled.*

Service stations

What we Christian ministers often fail to recognize is that we can serve others in many ways. Inviting a neighbor who lives alone to share a cup of coffee is a way of washing our neighbor's feet. Listening to a friend's tale of woe is an act of comfort. Likewise, merely being present to another is serving the other. And we must humble ourselves to be cared for by others, including Jesus.

> **JOHN 13:5** *[Jesus] poured water into a basin and began to wash the disciples' feet and to wipe them with the towel that was tied around him.*

On the road

❦ Health-conscious people may take a walk after eating a meal. Body movement aids digestion and alleviates drowsiness. A solitary walk offers Christian ministers the opportunity to reflect on the day and the different ways we have shared food with people. Unrecognized by Cleopas and his companion, Jesus joined them on their walk from Jerusalem to Emmaus and set their hearts afire. As they broke bread together, they realized who their traveling companion had been. He, however, disappeared. Reviewing the day's travels enables us to recognize Jesus in each person with whom we walked and dined. We may realize that meals and walks disclose our nearness to God.

> LUKE 24:30-31 *When [Jesus] was at the table with them, he took bread, blessed and broke it, and gave it to them. Then their eyes were opened, and they recognized him; and he vanished from their sight.*

God in the flesh

❦ Jesus showed us God in the only way that we could ever see God—in human flesh. Jesus' ministry of disclosing God is now entrusted to Christian ministry. We serve others because they, too, are reflections of God. It's often difficult to see God in the beggar on the steps or the homeless woman pushing her shopping cart. It's equally as difficult to see God in the wealthy drug addict or middle-class alcoholic. But in all people we serve, Jesus once again shows us God.

> JOHN 14:6 *"I am the way, and the truth, and the life. No one comes to the Father except through me."*

Branching out

Christian ministry is all about connections. This includes the many social service agencies that help us accomplish tasks like getting a homeless couple into a shelter, acquiring funding for programs, or providing food for the poor. But on a deeper level, ministry is about connecting to people at the source of their lives where God's grace in them meets God's grace in us. This type of relationship is like that between a vine and its branches: life flows and grows and produces abundantly. Jesus is the vine; ministers are branches who aid other branches in accepting the flow of graced life from God.

> **JOHN 15:5** *"I am the vine, you are the branches. Those who abide in me and I in them bear much fruit, because apart from me you can do nothing."*

CHAPTER 5

Holy Spirit

The animator of all life is the Holy Spirit, that mysterious person of the Trinity who has been imaged as fire and wind and tongues and doves and who is love and grace. Christian ministry has no effect without this giver-of-life who unites all creation into one. From the first verse of the Book of Genesis, when the "wind from God swept over the face of the waters" (1:3), to the last verse of the Book of Revelation, whose writer wishes "the grace of the Lord Jesus" (22:21) to everyone, the Holy Spirit brings order out of chaos. We live in the age of the Spirit, in which the Paraclete organizes the chaos of everyone's life, often choosing Christian ministers to be the instruments.

Pillar of fire

❦ Sometime the Spirit's work in the life of a minister is like that of fire. First, the Spirit sparks enthusiasm in us. Then, the Spirit ignites us so that we are compelled to follow God's desire. Our light draws people to the divine light. The Spirit's fire demands that it be shared, so we often divide our light, which is not dimmed as it is shared. Indeed, it becomes a pillar of fire leading people to God.

> ACTS 2:3 *Divided tongues, as of fire, appeared among [the apostles], and a tongue rested on each of them.*

The Spirit blows where it will

❦ The Paraclete blows you into places God wants you to be. Like a mysterious wind whose source no one knows, the Spirit pushes you to talk to strangers, visit the dying, counsel the wayward, and more. Sometimes all it takes is a gentle breeze to guide you in the direction of the Spirit. Other times it takes a tornado to move you to the right place. But if order, direction, and a sense of purpose are the results of your ministry, be assured that the wind of the Spirit has been pushing you along.

> ACTS 2:2 *Suddenly from heaven there came a sound like the rush of a violent wind, and it filled the entire house where [the apostles] were sitting.*

Let the reign begin

❦ Empowerment for ministry comes directly from the Holy Spirit. The Gospel of Mark depicts the beginning of Jesus' ministry with the story of his baptism in the Jordan River, the ripping apart of the heavens, and the descent of the Spirit upon him in the form of a dove. That Spirit drove Jesus into the wilderness for his 40-day fast. The Spirit-dove not only anointed Jesus for his public ministry but also announced that God's reign had begun.

> **MARK 1:10** *Just as [Jesus] was coming up out of the water, he saw the heavens torn apart and the Spirit descending like a dove on him.*

Learning God's language

Miscommunication brings chaos, and God is interested in creating order out of the chaos of our lives. At Pentecost, God reversed the story of Babel (Genesis 11:1-9) and enabled people to understand one another through the work of the Spirit. We Christian ministers continue God's orderly work every time we speak the language of the people to whom we minister.

> **ACTS 2:8** *[The Jews asked,] "How is it that we hear, each of us, in our own native language?"*

Come to Life

When two people say to each other, "I love you," they establish a bond, a relationship. The Spirit is the bond or relationship that exists between the Father and the Son in the Trinity—a bond so intense that it generates another whole person, the Holy Spirit. The best way to understand this mystery is to reflect on how the love between a man and a woman can bring a child to life. The love of the Father and Son brings into being the Holy Spirit. And this is the Spirit who breathes life into our ministry.

> **1 JOHN 4:13** *By this we know that we abide in [God] and he in us, because he has given us of his Spirit.*

God for us

❦ Only the author of John's gospel refers to the Holy Spirit as *Paraclete*, a word meaning "advocate," "lawyer," or "one who pleads a cause." In fact, in John's Gospel the Paraclete is Jesus risen from the dead, the reality of his new presence with his followers. Just as he represented his followers before his death, Jesus continues to do so after his resurrection. He does it for us every time we serve as advocates for the homeless or lawyers for the falsely accused or counselors to the oppressed or afflicted. Christian ministry is, simply put, pleading the cause of another.

> **JOHN 14:16** *"I will ask the Father, and he will give you another Advocate, to be with you forever."*

Stay connected

❦ When we walk into a dark room and turn on a lamp, we expect a light bulb to be illumined by electricity. If no light comes, the first thing we do is check the plug to see if it is connected to the source of electricity—the outlet in the wall. The Spirit is like the outlet. The Spirit is our connection to God. As long as we ministers are plugged in, we are doing what God is directing through the Spirit and our light is brightening the lives of others. If we are disconnected, we are unable to shed the light of God's love on those to whom we minister.

> **JOHN 14:17** *"This is the Spirit of truth, whom the world cannot receive, because it neither sees him nor knows him. You know him, because he abides with you, and he will be in you."*

Gifts to be given away

❦ The Spirit bestows gifts that are to be used for the common good. The gift of being able to listen to others intently as a minister has not been given to you for your good but for the good of others. Likewise, your gift of expressing in words the feelings of another is to be shared. Any spiritual gift given to you as a minister must be given away if you are to retain it.

> **1 CORINTHIANS 12:7** *To each is given the manifestation of the Spirit for the common good.*

Bound for freedom

❦ Christ's death and resurrection has freed us from the human constraints of sin and enables us to follow God—who is pure love. We are bound to God through Jesus Christ, and our freedom is found in that bond of love. The Paraclete gives ministers strength to facilitate the journey of others to that same freedom.

> **2 CORINTHIANS 3:17** *Now the Lord is the Spirit, and where the Spirit of the Lord is, there is freedom.*

Help in being heard

❦ Oftentimes when we're overwhelmed by our work, exhausted, and confused by the problems set before us, we ministers simply don't know what to say to God or how to say it. That's when the Spirit helps us formulate our prayers to God. The Spirit gives breath to our deepest longings and communicates our needs to God who, as it happens, already knows what we need.

> **ROMANS 8:26** *The Spirit helps us in our weakness; for we do not know how to pray as we ought, but that very Spirit intercedes with sighs too deep for words.*

Spiritual maintenance

❦ We often hit dry patches in our ministry. Spiritual dryness can be the result of a process of transition from one form of ministry to another; or it can be an indication that we need to take a day off, go on a vacation, or make a retreat. In the state of dryness, however, we discover our need for the Holy Spirit, the giver of life, who turns our dead-tiredness into living energy and quenches our parched spirits with living water.

> **JOHN 7:37-39** *"Let anyone who is thirsty come to me, and let the one who believes in me drink." Now he said this about the Spirit, which believers in him were to receive.*

Life-giver

❦ The Holy Spirit, who dwells in people, activates their gifts, and teaches them to pray, also broods over them, commissions them for action, and leads them to solitude and silence. Christian ministers who are attuned to the wind and breath of the Spirit have experienced the Paraclete in most—if not all—of these ways. In moments of solitude, the Spirit calls us out of ourselves and permits us "to see God." In times of silence, the Spirit nudges us away from our concerns and lets us "hear God." We are carried to another plane of existence in which we are aware that we are aware and experience simultaneously our humility and glory. For a fleeting moment, we are plunged even more deeply into the source of all life: the Holy Spirit.

> **ROMANS 5:5** *God's love has been poured into our hearts through the Holy Spirit that has been given to us.*

Returned Spirit

In Luke's Gospel, Jesus' final words, "Father, into your hands I commend my spirit" (23:46), serve as a model for every minister. At the end of every day, at the end of every life, we return to God the gift that has connected us to God throughout our lives—namely, God's very Spirit within us. Jesus' returning of his Spirit to the Father was his act of absolute trust in God and represented the culmination of his life's work. Our daily offering of the Spirit of Jesus back to God enables us to grow in our trust of the God into whose hands we will commend our own spirits on the last day of our lives.

LUKE 4:14 *Then Jesus, filled with the power of the Spirit, returned to Galilee, and a report about him spread through all the surrounding country.*

Raised Spirit

The Spirit who made possible Jesus' conception, the Spirit who filled him and guided him throughout his life, the Spirit whom he returned to his Father before he died, also raised Jesus to new life. The author of Luke's Gospel understands Jesus' resurrection to be like that of a spirited body, and in moments of transcendence we get a little taste of that new life awaiting us. For what the Spirit did for Jesus, the Spirit will do for us as well. We, too, will be absolutely, purely transformed.

ROMANS 1:4 *[Jesus Christ] was declared to be Son of God with power according to the spirit of holiness by resurrection from the dead.*

CHAPTER 6

Prayer

We busy ministers had better be prayerful ministers if we want to find satisfaction in our work and watch God multiply our efforts. No matter how we define it, prayer along the journey of life is the way we connect to God, the way we learn both to give and to receive. Grace flows during prayer. Sin is eliminated. And Jesus becomes the model of our prayer. No matter how many people he called, no matter how many infirm he healed, no matter how many sermons he delivered, Jesus took time to pray. We cannot minister in his name and not follow his example.

Feel the presence of God

❦ Some people define prayer as being in the presence of God. That's a helpful definition, since we are in God's presence whether we are aware of it or not. So, in a sense, we are praying at all times. There is not a single aspect of our ministry that we do—preaching, counseling, comforting, healing—when God is not with us.

EPHESIANS 6:18 *Pray in the Spirit at all times in every prayer and supplication.*

Pay attention

❦ God is always present to us. It's one of the unique qualities of divinity. However, in our busyness, we ministers are not always present to God. Our prayer can become like the telephone conversation we have while fixing dinner or washing dishes. With one ear to the phone we say, "Uh-huh," without a notion of what the other person just said. We pretend to be present to the other when, in fact, we are distracted and far away. Being present to God means that we set aside our busyness, put down the telephone, and give God our full attention.

LUKE 6:12 *Now during those days [Jesus] went out to the mountain to pray; and he spent the night in prayer to God.*

Praise

❦ In our moments of prayer we offer praise for what God is doing through our ministry. Creating a litany of praise is a way to make ourselves aware of all that God does for us and through us. Our being with those mourning the death of a loved one is God being present to them through us. Our working hard on a homily or class that we are preparing to give and our trying to discover new life in our tired words is God speaking through us. Each verse of our prayer should begin with, "Praise to you, God, for . . . ."

COLOSSIANS 4:2 *Devote yourselves to prayer, keeping alert in it with thanksgiving.*

Hear us, O Lord

Ministers are always asking God to guide a gathering, to bless a meal, to instill the right words, to be with someone, to protect a traveler. Many times we petition God for what others need in their sickness, loneliness, or transition. People say to us, "Pray for me," and we know that we have more to request of God. We can begin by saying, "God, hear all the needs that have been expressed to me today," and then continue by enumerating the most pressing of them.

PHILIPPIANS 4:6 *Do not worry about anything, but in everything by prayer and supplication with thanksgiving let your requests be made known to God.*

Please wait

Being able to wait is a form of prayer. After praising or petitioning, ministers often stand before God and wait and wait and wait. The act of waiting, of being quietly patient and not speaking another word, is its own form of prayer. God is not like a soda machine that gives you the soft drink you selected immediately after you deposit your coins. God is more like an e-mail correspondent who replies to your urgent missive on his or her own time.

ROMANS 12:12 *Rejoice in hope, be patient in suffering, persevere in prayer.*

Well-received gifts

❦ Another form of prayer is receiving. When we ministers receive anything, we should do so graciously. If God offers us a response, a new challenge, an insight, we must accept it in all humility. We do not deserve it, nor can we earn it. Our prayer can only be one of acceptance. This is most difficult for those of us who think that we owe everyone a favor for a favor, a gift for a gift, a thank-you note for a thank-you note. In fact, we often think of ourselves as givers instead of receivers. We listen to others, we preach, we teach, we do, we give of ourselves. But God balances this ministerial giving with all the blessings we receive.

> **MARK 11:24** *"Whatever you ask for in prayer, believe that you have received it, and it will be yours."*

Our Father

❦ The Lord's Prayer can help us articulate our own prayer. We begin with an addressee. In the Lord's Prayer, that addressee is "Father." (It could just as well be "Mother.") Addressing God in prayer is like writing a name on an envelope before mailing it. The name tells the post office to whom the letter needs to be delivered. Saying "Our Father" or "Our Mother" indicates that our prayer is headed to a real person, one who loves us unconditionally.

> **ISAIAH 63:16** *You, O LORD, are our father; our Redeemer from of old is your name.*

In heaven

❦ Before a letter can be delivered to an addressee, it needs a two-line address. By writing the street or post office box, and the city, state, and zip code, we give specific directions where the letter is to be delivered. Likewise, in the Lord's Prayer we declare that God lives in heaven. While we usually think upward when we hear the word "heaven," we know that heaven is not a place but a way of being. People of the ancient world thought in terms of a three-storied universe: heaven, where God lived; earth, where people lived; and *sheol,* or the underworld, where the dead lived. But heaven is wherever God is, and God is everywhere.

> **JONAH 2:7** *As my life was ebbing away, I remembered the LORD; and my prayer came to you, into your holy temple.*

Holy name

 We join the people to whom we minister in praying "Our Father." The emphasis is on the "our," indicating that God claims all people as children. God does not discriminate based on whether people are Jewish, Christian, Muslim, Buddhist, Hindu, or Taoist. From God's point of view, people are described in one collective word—children. God hears all children's prayers, no matter what name they use for the divine reality.

> **PSALM 84:8** *O LORD God of hosts, hear my prayer; give ear, O God of Jacob!*

The reign is at hand

 When we ministers pray the Lord's Prayer, we ask that God's reign will come on earth, as it already is in heaven. Jesus awakened people to the coming of God's reign primarily through parables about common things like yeast, lamps, and fig trees. The writers of the gospels used signs, like ripped-apart heavens or a torn Temple curtain, to declare that God's reign had already begun. If all the people of the earth would accept God as ruler of the world, the result would be absolute freedom, justice, and love. All people would see themselves as equal children of God—dedicated to serving one another, with no one having power over anyone else.

> **Sirach 35:21-22** *The prayer of the humble pierces the clouds, and it will not rest until it reaches its goal; it will not desist until the Most High responds and does justice for the righteous, and executes judgment.*

Your will, not mine

When we ask that God's will be done, we put ourselves at God's disposal. We make ourselves absolutely vulnerable in the presence of the divine. It is like the vulnerability that a husband and wife experience throughout their marriage as each shares the depths of who he or she is with the other. In the exchange, each stands in complete humility before the sacred presence of the other and puts himself or herself at the other's service. So do we ministers who do the will of God appear before those to whom we minister.

> **Sirach 35:20** *The one whose service is pleasing to the Lord will be accepted, and his prayer will reach to the clouds.*

Daily bread

The bread ministers eat does not always have physically nutritional value. More often than not, we eat of the God-filled lives of the people to whom we minister. We offer to others a morsel of our lives, and we receive in turn a crumb of theirs. Both they and we are fed, and the exchange becomes a sign of God living and working in all of our lives.

> **Matthew 21:22** *"Whatever you ask for in prayer with faith, you will receive."*

Forgiveness—given and received

Before true prayer can take place, reconciliation must occur between those who are estranged or in some kind of conflict. "Forgive us our sins as we forgive those who sin against us," we say in the Lord's Prayer. That makes it clear that receiving forgiveness is reciprocal—in the act of asking God to forgive us, we must also be asking others to forgive us. And to receive forgiveness, we have to offer forgiveness. Mediating the dialectic of forgiveness is a challenge faced by every Christian minister. Ministry is a lifetime process of resolving conflict, healing estrangement, and uniting divisions.

> **1 John 1:9** *If we confess our sins, he who is faithful and just will forgive us our sins and cleanse us from all unrighteousness.*

No test

It seems that humans are always trying to pass a test. It's a standard requirement to pass from one grade to another. Colleges thrive on giving tests to students during finals week. Add to these tests driver's tests, eye tests, physical exams, and all the other tests people give to others. No wonder we ask God not to put us to the test. Human tests are difficult enough to bear—how could we possibly withstand a test of our love for the divine?

> **Psalm 102:1** *Hear my prayer, O Lord; let my cry come to you.*

Delivered from evil

The last petition in the Lord's Prayer asks God to deliver us from all evil—that silent, invisible force that can lead us the wrong way. The image of evil—the devil in a red suit with cloven hooves for feet, horns on his head, a pitchfork in one hand, and a tail attached to his backside—is not the reality of evil, which can so possess people that they believe they are achieving good through killing, stealing, and hurting others. Because evil is so insidious, we pray that God will deliver us from it and not let it blind us to what God wills for our lives.

> **1 PETER 3:12** *The eyes of the Lord are on the righteous, and his ears are open to their prayer. But the face of the Lord is against those who do evil.*

CHAPTER 7

Baptism

Baptism is the one sacrament accepted by all Christians. No matter how ministers administer it—by pouring, sprinkling, dunking—Baptism serves to initiate people into the body of Christ, which is made up of all the churches or denominations who baptize in the name of the Father, Son, and Holy Spirit. The water used in the sacrament both signifies and accomplishes what is taking place in the person being baptized. He or she is washed clean of sin and plunged into the new life of a community of faith. Dying in the depths of the water, the individual rises reborn as a child in God's family. The reason that the sacrament of Baptism can never be repeated is that the relationships it establishes last forever.

Welcome to the family

❧ Baptism is a sacrament of initiation. That is, people are formally counted among the membership of the church only after they have undergone the ritual of initiation. Therefore, Christian ministers conduct this rite of passage with all the seriousness it demands. Through our action of cleansing the initiated with water, the person being initiated passes from the status of "outsider" to that of "insider." A new member of the body of Christ has been born, and thus the whole group has been changed.

> **MARK 10:38** *[Jesus said to James and John,] "Are you able to drink the cup that I drink, or be baptized with the baptism that I am baptized with?"*

Cross the threshold

❧ A threshold is another name for a point of entrance. We ministers don't give much thought to all the doors we pass through on any given day, but we do enter through the doors of homes, cars, hospitals, businesses, schools, churches, etc. Every door is a threshold to the world of the people who live or work on the other side. That is why Baptism is a threshold experience. Just as the Israelites escaped from slavery to freedom by walking through the water of the Sea of Reeds, so do we assist others in passing through the waters of the baptismal font to a new life in the community that professes faith in Jesus Christ.

> **LUKE 12:50** *"I have a baptism with which to be baptized, and what stress I am under until it is completed!"*

The source of life

❧ Water is everywhere. Streams and rivers wind through the countryside, leaving behind their hidden sources. Water falls out of the sky as clouds turn loose their moisture and wash the earth with freshness and life. If we go to a lake or ocean, we can't help but stick in a hand or toe. Water elicits a primal response from deep inside us. It wants to connect us to its flow, and we want to be a part of it. No wonder we baptize with water.

> **REVELATION 22:17** *Let everyone who is thirsty come. Let anyone who wishes take the water of life as a gift.*

Triune love

❧ Not only does Baptism welcome people into the Christian community, but it simultaneously establishes them in relationship to the three persons of the Trinity. The love of the Father eternally begets the Son, and the love between them generates the Spirit. Baptism enables all believers to share in that triad of love-relationships. And it is our continued experience of the love-filled embrace of Father, Son, and Spirit that keeps transforming us into the ministers we are destined to be.

> **MATTHEW 28:19** *"Go . . . and make disciples of all nations, baptizing them in the name of the Father and of the Son and of the Holy Spirit."*

Dressed in white

❧ In the spring, people go shopping for new clothes. They buy garments sewn from white or pastel-colored cloth that reflects the new life of the season. When the newly baptized are raised out of the font, they are also draped with a white cloth as a sign of their

Christian dignity, purity, and newness. For the same reason, the church uses a white pall at funerals to signify that the life of dying and rising begun on the day of Baptism is only complete with final death and resurrection. It is our job as ministers to make this birth-death-life connection for people.

> **GALATIANS 3:27** *As many of you as were baptized into Christ have clothed yourselves with Christ.*

Candlelight

Have you noticed all the new sections displaying candles in greeting-card shops, grocery stores, and arts and crafts stores? It's difficult to find a home today without a candle or two displayed and burned for various occasions. The interesting thing about a candle is that it is most itself when fire is consuming it. That's why we give people a candle after they are baptized that has been ignited from the Easter Candle, a sign of the risen Christ. We are telling the newly baptized that they will be most themselves if they let their light shine, even as it consumes them into new life.

> **REVELATION 21:23** *The city has no need of sun or moon to shine on it, for the glory of God is its light, and its lamp is the Lamb.*

Be like Christ

It's applied to a baby's bottom. It's rubbed into aching joints and muscles by athletes. It's slathered on before we spend time in the sun. Oil, no matter what its form, protects and heals us. That's why we smear it on the heads of the newly baptized. It anoints them to be like the *Messiah* or *Christ* (the Hebrew and Greek words for "anointed"). In other words, the person who is anointed with chrism oil, blessed once a year by a bishop, is "Christened." He or she becomes a verb, a Christ-person living his or her life for others.

MARK 1:1 *The beginning of the good news of Jesus Christ, the Son of God.*

A part of the whole

People don't give a lot of thought to the various parts of their bodies until one of them has a problem. They take their body unity for granted because they know that hands touch, feet walk, legs support, arms reach outward, the heart pumps, the kidneys purify, etc. Baptism, however, adds the bodies of the newly baptized to the body of Christ, an ever-expanding and integrating organism headed by Jesus. Christian ministers serve that body—both as a whole and as individuals. Thus, by feeding one hungry member, we feed all the members. By guiding all wayward members, we guide each individual.

ROMANS 12:5 *We, who are many, are one body in Christ, and individually we are members one of another.*

A matter of life and death

Baptism is about dying—going under the water in the font. It is also about rising—being raised up to a process of overflowing life. The rhythm of dying and rising begun in Baptism imitates Jesus' death and resurrection, and it lasts a lifetime. Once Christians go into the waters and emerge again, they are never the same again. They've experienced both death and resurrection. This interplay between death and life characterizes the lives of all the baptized, but especially those of ministers. We are responsible for showing the rest how to sway to the rhythm graciously and gracefully.

ROMANS 6:3-4 *Do you not know that all of us who have been baptized into Christ Jesus were baptized into his death? Therefore we have been buried with him by baptism into death, so that, just as Christ was raised from the dead by the glory of the Father, so we too might walk in newness of life.*

CHAPTER 8

Confirmation

Many Christians celebrate the sacrament of initiation called Confirmation, Chrismation, or Commissioning. Confirmation is seen as sealing what was done at Baptism, and it takes many forms. For adults baptized as infants, it presents the opportunity of affirming publicly what others declared for them previously. For newly baptized adults, it signifies their reception of the gifts of the Holy Spirit. And for teenagers, it is seen as a rite of passage, much like their later graduations from grade school, high school, or college. No matter when it is done or under what circumstances, however, Confirmation, like Baptism, is permeated by the Holy Spirit, who offers nothing but spiritual gifts.

The property of . . .

❦ In the ancient world, slaves were sealed or tattooed on the fore-head with a sign indicating to whom they belonged. The Holy Spirit, who gives Christians new life in Baptism, tattoos them in Confirmation as servants of one another. We Christian ministers, therefore, should be servants par excellence of others, models of how other followers of Jesus should serve one another through prayer and deed, for in serving others we serve Christ.

> **REVELATION 7:4** *I heard the number of those who were sealed, one hundred forty-four thousand, sealed out of every tribe of the people of Israel.*

The gift of wisdom

❦ In the process of being sealed with the Holy Spirit, all Christians are given the gift of wisdom. This wisdom is not the type of wisdom a person gets after going to school. It is more like the wisdom witnessed in the elderly—the ability to judge rightly and follow a sound course of action based on knowledge, experience, and understanding. We ministers use the Holy Spirit's gift of wisdom when we assist others in solving their problems, when we challenge the world-view of our hearers, when we witness to the values of family, honesty, and generosity with our lifestyle. Wisdom enables us to penetrate whatever is true and lasting.

> **JAMES 1:5** *If any of you is lacking in wisdom, ask God, who gives to all generously and ungrudgingly, and it will be given you.*

Understanding the ways of God

✿ Closely associated with wisdom is the Spirit's gift of understanding. Ministers familiar with this gift know that it means seeing how the ways of God can operate in ordinary lives. Those who minister to patients in a hospital, for example, try to help them discern the meaning of their suffering. Those who work with couples considering divorce attempt to assist both sides to understand the importance of reconciliation—even if a divorce takes place. What ministers do is help others draw out the meaning of God's often contradictory presence in their lives.

> **1 JOHN 5:20** *We know that the Son of God has come and has given us understanding so that we may know him who is true; and we are in him who is true, in his Son Jesus Christ.*

Right turns

✿ The Holy Spirit offers to each person the ability to render justice. This gift has little to do with legal justice. The Spirit's gift is biblical justice, which does what is right because it is the right thing to do, whether it is required by law or not. And yet, as any minister knows, there are times when the right thing to do is to do nothing. It takes the Spirit's gift of right judgment to know what the right thing really is.

> **JOHN 7:24** *"Do not judge by appearances, but judge with right judgment."*

Courage

✿ The Holy Spirit's gift of courage is the ability to face and deal with anything along life's continuum that is dangerous, difficult, or painful. One who has not accepted the gift of courage withdraws from the challenge of living. The Christian minister who leads others where they sometimes prefer not to go is an example of the Spirit's gift of courage. None of us is ever alone in facing anything or anyone. God's Spirit is with us through the gift of courage.

> **WISDOM 8:7** *If anyone loves righteousness, her labors are virtues; for she teaches self-control and prudence, justice and courage; nothing in life is more profitable for mortals than these.*

Knowledge

The Spirit's gift of knowledge enables us to know ourselves and to know others, and thus we are able to gain knowledge of the God who lives within every human being. When we minister to others, we leave knowing God better that ever. And that is when we have begun to use fully the gift of knowledge.

> **2 PETER 1:2** *May grace and peace be yours in abundance in the knowledge of God and of Jesus our Lord.*

Real presence

Some people equate reverence with such activities as folding hands, bowing, kneeling, and genuflecting. But the Spirit's gift of reverence pushes ministers to recognize much more deeply the honor and dignity due every human person. Reverence removes our filtering categories of race, gender, sexual orientation, financial status, etc. The Holy Spirit instead engenders in us a deep respect, love, and appreciation for every person as an image of God. And it is then our responsibility to teach others that real reverence is about how we treat others.

EPHESIANS 5:21 *Be subject to one another out of reverence for Christ.*

Wonder and awe

✻ The gift of being able to stand before a sunrise over the ocean or snow-covered mountain summits and be so caught up in the experience that we lose track of time, place, and self is a manifestation of the gift of the Spirit's gift of wonder and awe. The transcendence we ministers experience—that is, the feeling of being lifted up to see reality from a broader perspective—is a moment of worship, a recognition that God is God and we are mere human beings animated by the Spirit's life-giving gifts.

HABAKKUK 3:2 *O LORD, I have heard of your renown, and I stand in awe, O LORD, of your work.*

CHAPTER 9

Eucharist

Some people call the Eucharist simply "breaking bread." Others refer to it as the "Lord's Supper" or "Mass." No matter what it is called, however, for ministers the Eucharist is the central act of Christian liturgical life. The word *eucharist* means "thanksgiving," and when we celebrate the Eucharist we are giving thanks for the sum total of all God's blessings that the entire body of Christ has received. Ministers set the table; prepare the food; and take, bless, break, and invite the community of believers to share it, themselves, and Jesus Christ with one another.

Take action

❦ The first action of Eucharist for ministers is taking. We probably think immediately that we take food—bread, and wine—drink. And we do. But there is more taking that goes on when we celebrate the Eucharist. We take people, represented by the bread and wine, into our hands. The fact that people present themselves before us in prayer is a demonstration of their willingness to be food for one another. It's the same thing families do when they gather for a meal on Thanksgiving Day, Christmas, or Easter.

> **MARK 14:22** *[Jesus] took a loaf of bread, and after blessing it he broke it, gave it to [his disciples], and said, "Take; this is my body."*

Bless us, O Lord

❦ Gathered around tables in their homes, many families pray over their food, thanking God for their bounty and invoking God to bless those who are preparing to share the gifts they are about to receive. Once blessed, food is treated with greater respect because it represents all those gathered around the table. Blessed food shared by blessed people around blessed tables is Eucharist.

> **1 CORINTHIANS 10:16** *The cup of blessing that we bless, is it not a sharing in the blood of Christ? The bread that we break, is it not a sharing in the body of Christ?*

Break and broken

❦ In usual usage, "broken" implies "useless." A broken leg keeps a table from serving its purpose. A broken base keeps the lamp from gracing us with light. But broken food is different. The action of breaking enables all to share. Ministers take food, bless it, and break it. In a similar way, people must be broken if they are to be shared. They must be broken out of their shells and narrow self-interests and old ways of doing things. Those who minister are entrusted with the sacred action of breaking open the lives of others.

> **LUKE 22:19** *[Jesus] took a loaf of bread, and when he had given thanks, he broke it and gave it to [his disciples], saying, "This is my body, which is given for you. Do this in remembrance of me."*

Share and share alike

After food is taken, blessed, and broken, all that remains is the sharing. That means that it is eaten. During the Eucharist, a small particle of bread and a sip of wine suffice. However, when families gather, more is needed. All members usually are seated around one large table. They begin sharing their lives through conversation. Then they pass around platters of food and containers of beverages. As they eat and drink, in a sense they feast on one another. No one goes home hungry. The bonds of family have been recognized in the breaking and sharing that took place with the meal.

> **JOHN 6:11** *Jesus took the loaves, and when he had given thanks, he distributed them to those who were seated; so also the fish, as much as they wanted.*

Body of Christ

Why do Christians take, bless, break, and share? Because we need to manifest to one another who we are: the body of Christ. Human beings don't merely inhabit a physical body; each of us belongs to a series of bodies, groups through whom we disclose who we are. During a family meal, for example, the members are drawn into the action of taking, blessing, breaking, and sharing. Gathered around a table, they manifest who they are as a family unit. Gathered around the Lord's table, we, as members of a church, manifest who we are. Thus, the body of Christ is not only *on* the altar, but it is *around* the altar.

> **1 CORINTHIANS 12:27** *Now you are the body of Christ and individually members of it.*

Welcome home

The body of Christ that gathers around the altar at church engages in fellowship by greeting one another. Some people refer to the action of opening the door into the church and saying "Hello" or "Good morning" as hospitality. It is the same hospitality we offer when friends or family members arrive at the front door of our homes. We open the portal with welcomes, hugs, handshakes, greetings. We renew the ties that bind us as family. Christian ministers assume a greater task in facilitating the welcoming of those who come to worship. For we greet not only the members of the church as individuals, but we welcome everyone as members of the body of Christ. Through the Eucharist, we will make visible our common identity.

> **ROMANS 15:7** *Welcome one another . . . just as Christ has welcomed you, for the glory of God.*

Mea culpa

No minister is worthy to be a member of the body of Christ, much less to lead others in the action of manifesting it. Often we ministers separate ourselves from the whole. Our unbridled desires hurt other members. Our words strip others of their reputation. Thoughts that we are somehow better than others can lead to dissension in our congregations. We are supposed to facilitate the reconciliation of the members of the body of Christ, but we must start with ourselves. We need to ask that others forgive our weaknesses, as we declare that all of us are sinners.

2 Corinthians 5:18 *All this is from God, who reconciled us to himself through Christ, and has given us the ministry of reconciliation.*

Let us pray

For ministers, part of the act of gathering the members of the body of Christ in Eucharist is leading prayer. This is a heavy responsibility, for we are called upon to be the voice of the whole. Usually with heads bowed, we lead the assembly into a communion of prayer. We summarize the prayer of all into one petition to which all give their assent, saying, "Amen."

1 Corinthians 12:14 *Indeed, the body does not consist of one member but of many.*

Word of the Lord

One medium of communication is the spoken word, which can be used to greet, praise, or condemn. Family members learn quickly that words spoken around a table can either facilitate or stunt the growth of all. So words must be chosen well and spoken with care. People likewise expect ministers to proclaim God's words with care and interpret them with grace.

John 1:1 *In the beginning was the Word, and the Word was with God, and the Word was God.*

Inspire and teach

❦ Some ministers call their opportunity to preach a "sermon," and others call it a "homily." What name we bestow on it, however, is not what makes it important. The key to preaching is preparation. Our awesome task is to build a bridge from a text that was written thousands of years ago to living people who are seated directly in front of us. It is no easy job to abstract God's message from the Scriptures and apply it to the lives of the members of the body of Christ today. Our helper and guide must be the Holy Spirit—the one who inspired the text and continues to inspire both lectors and preachers today.

> **2 TIMOTHY 3:16** *All scripture is inspired by God and is useful for teaching, for reproof, for correction, and for training in righteousness.*

We believe

❦ Every family has some type of code by which its members live. There may be simple verbal rules or beliefs articulated by the parents or formal written guidelines agreed upon by everyone. That code defines the lifestyle of the members of the family. In church, the equivalent of a code is called a creed. It articulates what the members believe, which in turn dictates how they live. A creed serves as a picture frame that encompasses a painting of the body of Christ. Without the frame, the church becomes amorphous, without shape, without identity, without lifestyle.

> **1 CORINTHIANS 12:18** *As it is, God arranged the members in the body, each one of them, as he chose.*

Hear our prayers

✤ Eucharist brings together lots of needy people, including Christian ministers, to intercede for one another. Members of families do this for one another. Siblings help one another by presenting a brother's or sister's concerns to their parents. Adults call upon other adults to help care for those in hospitals, the aging, and the dying. Ministers lead members of the body of Christ in doing the same. Our prayer for those in need should lead to action on their behalf. Otherwise, Eucharist has had no affect on us. The body invited to the table must be cared for by all.

PSALM 20:5B *May the LORD fulfill all your petitions.*

One bread

✤ Christians are bread for one another. Alone, one grain of wheat produces only a little flour dust. Ground together, however, many grains of wheat produce enough meal to make dough for bread. Carefully, the dough is kneaded, mixed again and again, until there is but one body of dough. Fired by electricity or gas it rises, bloated by the yeasty Spirit, and bakes into a loaf. The work of making bread is the work of making community, the work ministers must do to present Eucharist to God.

1 CORINTHIANS 10:17 *Because there is one bread, we who are many are one body for we all partake of the one bread.*

Fruit of the vine

✤ A glass of wine begins with single grapes in a community cluster. Chosen by the vineyard owner, clusters are robbed of their juice and squeezed until all that remains are seeds and skins. In vats, the juice begins to ferment. Then, at the right time, it is put in casks for aging. The wine of Eucharist represents both the work involved and the time it takes for the community to become one. Without the fermentation process, only grape juice remains. Without the Spirit, the community would never be poured into the world. Like fine wine, the blood of Christ inebriates all who drink of it.

> **1 CORINTHIANS 11:25** *[The Lord] took the cup, after supper, saying, "This cup is the new covenant in my blood. Do this, as often as you drink it, in remembrance of me."*

Gift offerings

✤ Those who do liturgy come with individual gifts bestowed upon them by the Spirit. Some are readers, some singers, some musicians, some preachers. The gifts of each are given for the good of the whole and are meant to be used to produce one body, signified by the bread and wine. The little contribution we ministers make is returned to us a hundredfold.

> **ROMANS 12:5** *We, who are many, are one body in Christ, and individually we are members one of another.*

Let us give thanks

✤ The purpose of making Eucharist is to say "thank you" to God. We ministers can easily miss the gifts that God gives to every one of us. Waking up from sleep is a gift, as is family, sunshine, green grass, snow, rain, work, etc. If we were aware of these many gifts, we would spend most of our day in a litany of thanksgiving to God. We can never finish offering our thanks, because the gifts continue to be lavished upon us. When we make Eucharist, we are joined by others who are as grateful as we are, and in one grand chorus we say thank you to our God, who never ceases to bestow gifts upon us beyond measure.

Revelation 7:12 *"Amen! Blessing and glory and wisdom and thanksgiving and honor and power and might be to our God forever and ever! Amen."*

Grateful acclamation

As a minister, be thankful for the holiness that God shares with you and every member of your congregation. Be thankful for the life, death, and resurrection of God's Son, Jesus Christ, who showed us how to live lives of thanksgiving. And be thankful for the accessibility to God that Jesus has provided. Your acclamations of praise can never adequately give thanks for God's grace in your life.

Revelation 19:5 *"Praise our God, all you his servants, and all who fear him, small and great."*

Come Holy Spirit

When we ministers celebrate the Eucharist, we call upon the Holy Spirit to work in and through every person we lead in prayer. Just as the Spirit overshadowed the Virgin Mary and she conceived Jesus, so God's Spirit breathes divine life into people so that, in the words of Saint Augustine of Hippo, they become who they already are: the body of Christ. In sharing the bread and cup, they share one another and become more and more like Christ.

1 Corinthians 12:13 *In the one Spirit we were all baptized into one body—Jews or Greeks, salves or free—and we were all made to drink of one Spirit.*

The Last Supper remembered

❧ No one knows exactly what Jesus said or did on the night before he died. We know he ate a Passover meal with his friends, but each gospel portrays the details of the Last Supper in a different manner. In Mark's gospel, for example, Jesus refers to the cup of the covenant; in Matthew's, Jesus offers a cup for the forgiveness of sins; and in Luke's, Jesus calls it the cup of the new covenant, as Paul does in his First Letter to the Corinthians (11:23-26). But despite these minor differences, it is clear that the Passover meal was transformed by Jesus' followers into a way to remember his death and resurrection. Although the details surrounding family meals at Thanksgiving, Christmas, and Easter can be murky, the stories of memorable dinners and parties bring family members unity. So does the narrative of the Lord's Supper help make the members of Christ's body one.

> **MATTHEW 26:26-28** *Jesus took a loaf of bread, and after blessing it he broke it, gave it to the disciples, and said, "Take, eat; this is my body." Then he took a cup, and after giving thanks he gave it to them, saying, "Drink from it, all of you; for this my blood of the covenant, which is poured out for many for the forgiveness of sins."*

Remember who we are

❧ The act of remembering, *anamnesis,* is crucial to any family. The collective remembering and retelling of family stories—usually at Thanksgiving, Christmas, and Easter—serves as glue to hold its members together. During the eucharistic celebration, ministers lead the members of the church into a collective remembering of what God has done for humankind from the moment of creation. Remembering defines us as community—giving our history, revealing our roots, showing our connections. Eucharistic *anamnesis* reminds us that we are God's children.

2 TIMOTHY 2:8 *Remember Jesus Christ, raised from the dead, a descendant of David.*

Make God an offer

What can ministers offer to God, the source of all that is? Absolutely nothing. We can only offer what God has already given to us! And that is exactly what we do during Eucharist. Through our symbolic eating and drinking, we offer to God ourselves as members of Christ's body. Our offering reveals our care for ourselves, others, and the whole of creation. God always accepts our meager gifts, because God gave them to us in the first place. If we received the gifts with open hands, then God invites us to offer them back with open hands and not clenched fists.

HEBREWS 10:10 *It is by God's will that we have been sanctified through the offering of the body of Jesus Christ once for all.*

On one another's behalf

Ministers are not alone in making Eucharist. In fact, we are never alone, no matter how isolated we may attempt to be. Each of us is connected through blood to our immediate family and to our wider family circles. Each of us is also connected through our common humanity to all the living and dead. Eucharist binds all members of the body of Christ—present and past—in the act of petitioning God to aid all members of the church. We ministers lead this intercession and live it daily as we serve the members of our communities.

HEBREWS 7:25 *[Jesus] is able for all time to save those who approach God through him, since he always lives to make intercession for them.*

Praise the Lord

🌸 Only God is worthy of all praise, honor, and worship. And that is what Eucharist attempts to achieve: a perfect hymn of praise or *doxology*. Of course, being human means that we can never render anything perfectly to God. The best we can do, united as Christ's body and enlivened by the Spirit, is to voice our words of praise. We join men and women of the past and the present in words of praise that echo through millennia and whose sound waves bounce off planets light years away. The doxology is an opportunity for each of us to join in the chorus, to sing forever a song that can never adequately thank God for literally everything.

> **REVELATION 5:13** *To the one seated on the throne and to the Lamb be blessing and honor and glory and might forever and ever!*

The *paschal* in Paschal Mystery

🌸 Eucharist celebrates the Paschal Mystery of Jesus. *Paschal*, a word meaning "passover," refers first to the Israelites' coming face-to-face with death as Egyptian slaves and passing over to life through the Exodus. Like the Israelites, Jesus faced death but passed over to new life. During every Eucharist we remember Jesus' death and resurrection, his passover, even as we, members of his body, are engaged in our own passover, which began the day we were baptized.

> **LUKE 22:15** *"I have eagerly desired to eat this Passover with you before I suffer."*

The *mystery* in Paschal Mystery

❦ The word *mystery* usually refers to that which cannot be explained. But when we refer to Jesus' *Paschal Mystery*, we mean the events in his life wherein God was discovered to be at work. What the Paschal Mystery reveals is that God is present exactly where we would never have thought to look. For example, God is present in suffering. God is not masochistic, but God does suffer with people, revealing the divine presence in the human flesh of ill people as well as in those who aid them. God is also present in death, our last opportunity during this life to recognize the one who has sustained us.

> **1 CORINTHIANS 11:26** *As often as you eat this bread and drink the cup, you proclaim the Lord's death until he comes.*

The Body of Christ, Amen

❦ Our religious culture tends to reduce Eucharist to a Jesus-and-me moment. However, our very use of the word *amen* indicates that we are part of a bigger whole. Saying "amen," meaning "so be it," to the minister's statement, "The body of Christ" or "The blood of Christ," is our threefold consent to communion. First, we say that the bread is the body of Christ and the wine is the blood of Christ. Second, we say that each one of us, individual members of the church, is the body of Christ. And third, we say that together we are the body of Christ, visible to one another and to the world.

> **1 CORINTHIANS 12:12** *Just as the body is one and has many members, and all the members of the body, though many, are one body, so it is with Christ.*

Enter into ritual

❦ Eucharist, no matter in what church it is celebrated, involves some ritual, the step-by-step process that enables people to manifest who they are to one another and to the world. While ritual can become burdensome and defeat its intended purpose, usually it succeeds. Its success depends, however, upon the minister who leads it and the people who participate in it. Like family ritual, which sometimes degenerates into members of a family happening to eat together, eucharistic ritual needs the active participation of all. No one can predict the outcome of ritual. All we can do is enter into it.

> **SIRACH 50:19** *The people of the LORD Most High offered their prayers before the Merciful One, until the order of worship of the LORD was ended, and they completed his ritual.*

Our good work never ends

❦ Eucharist reminds ministers that all Christians are always in the process of becoming the body of Christ. We gather to make thanksgiving to God, and then we are sent out to live it in service to one another. Our service calls us back to celebrate and give thanks for God's work in our lives of service. This does nothing other than to empower us for more service. The body of Christ we were last week is not the same body we are this week. We have become more of who we already were. That alone is enough taste to make us desire more. This process of becoming will end only when Christ returns in glory.

> **1 CORINTHIANS 12:26** *If one member suffers, all suffer together with it; if one member is honored, all rejoice together with it.*

Emptiness required

❦ Service without Eucharist is like dinner without food. Our service to other members of Christ's body is what empties and prepares us to celebrate Eucharist and make manifest that body again and again. We come to Eucharist empty, hungry, ready to be filled with Christ and with one another.

> **PHILIPPIANS 2:7** *[Christ Jesus] emptied himself, taking the form of a slave, being born in human likeness.*

Go forth

❦ Ministers end the Eucharist with a commissioning. We send forth the assembly to manifest to others who we have just become: the body of Christ. We tell the others to go into the whole world and be Jesus for it. Yet that is a task that we ministers spend our lives embracing. Just when we think we have finished our mission to someone we realize that we are sent elsewhere and to someone else. Thus, the whole life of a minister is tied to Eucharist, mirroring for others how one is sent by the body of Christ to be its representative in the places where all the members cannot be.

> **2 CORINTHIANS 2:17** *We are not peddlers of God's word like so many; but in Christ we speak as persons of sincerity, as persons sent from God and standing in his presence.*

CHAPTER 10

Penance

S ome people call it *Confession*. Others refer to it as the sacrament of *Reconciliation*. Its official name, however, is *Penance*. "Confession" names only one part of the process—the acknowledgment of sin. "Reconciliation" describes the result of the celebration—the restoration of our estranged relationship with God and others. "Penance," however, describes the entire process whereby we reach reconciliation. The steps of this process include contrition, confession, satisfaction, and absolution. These are the same steps we follow in most of the meaningful relationships of our lives. In those relationships, we are always expressing sorrow, explaining why we did what we did, trying to make up for our behavior, and, we hope, receiving forgiveness from those we hurt. In Penance, we are doing the same, both with God and with the entire Christian community.

I have sinned

❦ Before we ministers can preach contrition, we must be contrite ourselves. We must first be aware that we are sinners—individually and collectively. Individually, we fail. We say the wrong words and hurt another. Collectively, we engage in behavior that estranges us from the other members of our church. Sin occurs when we are not who we are called to be, and its power is found in its ability to divide people. Sin can be overcome only when the human bond proves itself stronger than sin, and the way we do that is through acknowledging our faults and failings to one another. Vulnerability conquers sin. God works through our weakness to reverse estrangement and bring people together.

> **2 CORINTHIANS 12:9** *[The Lord] said to me, "My grace is sufficient for you, for power is made perfect in weakness."*

How God reconciles

❦ Jesus broke down the fences keeping people apart. He called the outcast and sinners to follow him, forming them into his body of believers, instilling in them the Spirit and giving them a vision of living as God's children. Jesus gave ministers the model for becoming instruments of God's healing and reconciling presence in the world. Through our work, God reconciles the world.

> **COLOSSIANS 1:20** *Through [Christ] God was pleased to reconcile to himself all things, whether on earth or in heaven, by making peace through the blood of his cross.*

Brought back to Baptism

❦ Another way to look at Penance is to see it through the lens of Baptism, the means through which Christians were initiated into the body of Christ. Because we are not perfect, we continue to fail; we do not always live up to our baptismal faith. Penance restores us to the original state of our Baptism. It enables us to begin again to continue our journey of lifetime conversion. We do not give up hope, because living a Christian life is a lifelong process of seeking pardon, experiencing forgiveness, and growing in relationship with God and others. So our Baptism is renewed regularly through our celebration of the sacrament of Penance.

> ACTS 15:3 *[Paul and Barnabas] were sent on their way by the church, and . . . they reported the conversion of the Gentiles, and brought great joy to all the believers.*

The ripple effect of sin

❦ Because we are the body of Christ, the reconciliation we establish with others is simultaneously enacted with God, and vice versa. That's why Penance is best celebrated in community. The hurt we caused to an individual usually has rippled toward others, who in some way participate in it. In a family, for example, anger spreads like wildfire. So not only do those who were upset with each other need to be reconciled, but they need to seek the pardon of the other members of the family. Likewise in church, we need to be restored to full communion with the other members and with God, who sustains the body of Christ with love.

> 2 CORINTHIANS 5:19 *In Christ God was reconciling the world to himself, not counting their trespasses against them, and entrusting the message of reconciliation to us.*

Heartily sorry

❦ Contrition indicates that we have learned from whatever we did. Genuine contrition begins in the heart and flows to every cell of the body. It forms us more and more into the image of Christ. It continues the process of conversion begun on the day of our Baptism. Coming from within us, contrition flows outward to others.

> **BARUCH 5:1** *Take off the garment of your sorrow and affliction, O Jerusalem, and put on forever the beauty of the glory from God.*

Confess to almighty God

The flow begun by contrition leads inexorably to confession of our sins. Such a confession may be generic, a simple acknowledgment that we are sinners, or it may be specific, a naming of the sins we accuse ourselves of having committed. Confession indicates that we have come to a point where we know ourselves and we know God, the merciful one. As we ministers listen to penitents confess their sins, we become the vehicles whereby God pronounces forgiveness. We declare that what God has done for each sinner God has done for the entire community.

> **1 JOHN 1:9** *If we confess our sins, he who is faithful and just will forgive us our sins and cleanse us from all unrighteousness.*

Satisfaction guaranteed

In our families we show the people we hurt that we are truly sorry by giving a small gift, saying a kind word, or doing a kind deed to demonstrate the conversion that has taken root in our life. Likewise, we ministers need to demonstrate our true contrition when we cause harm to the body of Christ. If we destroyed someone's reputation, for example, then some restoration is needed. If we failed to render justice, then it must be given. Such satisfaction is a remedy for our sins and a step toward our renewal of life. By altering our words or behavior, we renew the vision of our lifetime journey of conversion.

> **1 PETER 5:10** *After you have suffered for a little while, the God of all grace, who has called you to his eternal glory in Christ, will himself restore, support, strengthen, and establish you.*

You are absolved

To be absolved is to be forgiven with no strings attached. Only God absolves perfectly; people do so imperfectly. As ministers, all we can do is reach out to others and, in God's name, assure them that they are forgiven and will be healed.

> **SIRACH 2:11** *The LORD is compassionate and merciful; he forgives sins and saves in time of distress.*

At one with the community

We Christian ministers are one with our communities. By embracing our own sinfulness, we are able to forgive others. By showing our own contrition, we support others in their weakness. By rendering satisfaction ourselves, we build up what has been torn down. By forgiving others, we are forgiven.

> **JAMES 5:16** *Confess your sins to one another, and pray for one another, so that you may be healed.*

Let go

The process of Penance is based on God's call, which can be heard in the Scriptures. It's a call to come nearer to the source of all relationships, even as we recognize our unworthiness. We ministers do not condone sin, but neither do we let it get in our way. We do not excuse sin, but neither do we let it keep us from those we love. After hearing the word of God, we let go of our sin and that of others. All we have left is the word of forgiveness spoken by God, who calls us to a graceful conversion for the rest of our lives.

> **HEBREWS 11:1-2** *Long ago God spoke to our ancestors in many and various ways by the prophets, but in these last days he has spoken to us by a Son.*

Be not afraid

We ministers must let go of our sin so that our truest selves can emerge. We must realize that we are children of God and that just as we forgive others from the depths of who we are, God forgives us from within the depths of God's mystery. At the moment of forgiveness, our lives are flooded with more grace, and we realize that we have nothing left to fear.

> **2 CORINTHIANS 5:21** *For our sake [God] made him to be sin who knew no sin, so that in him we might become the righteousness of God.*

CHAPTER 11

Anointing the Sick

Any kind of illness causes isolation. Those who are sick withdraw from others to harness their energy and focus on healing. This further isolates them from the groups with whom they associate. Even a dripping nose or watery eyes can cause someone to want to stay home, and serious illness or physical pain can make it almost impossible to be out and about. The confines imposed by some types of treatment for mental illness certainly keeps people away from others. For ministers, then, one of the primary purposes of Anointing the Sick is to dissipate this isolation and remind people that they are still members of the body of Christ, the church, the community of believers.

Human ills

❧ One aspect of being human is getting ill. At one time or another, everyone discovers that he or she is suffering from something as simple as the common cold to something as serious as cancer. As the human body ages, the ability to replace worn-out cells diminishes. Viruses attack what may have been a system fairly immune to disease. Ultimately, the human condition sets in. The battles a person may have been able to mount against sickness in younger years are lost in the weakness of older years. Ministers know that sickness is not a punishment for sin but rather another aspect of being human—like loving, eating, dying. And just as God is discovered at work in other human activities, so is the divine present when people are ill.

> **JOHN 11:4** *"This illness does not lead to death; rather it is for God's glory, so that the Son of God may be glorified through it."*

Healthy touches

❧ While the human condition involves illness, people do not submit to it willingly. Ministers join family members, doctors, and scientists in the fight against all disease and in assisting the sick in seeking the blessings of good health. Keeping in mind the wholeness of every person, we begin to see that separating physical relief from spiritual comfort is merely a mental exercise. Ministering to the physical is serving the spiritual and vice versa. The presence of God is manifest in the hands of a skilled physician as well as in the hands of the minister who offers a healing touch. Anointing the Sick treats the whole person.

> **PSALM 41:3** *The LORD sustains [those who consider the poor] on their sickbed; in their illness you heal all their infirmities.*

Soothing oils

❦ Just as people of the past sought to soothe the pain of those who were suffering by anointing them with salves, oils, and ointments, this practice continues today. If we burn a finger, we put some type of oily substance on it. If a son or daughter scrapes a knee, we apply an ointment on the wound. If we spend too much time in the sun, we apply a healing oil to our burned skin. When we ministers anoint the sick with oil, not only are we promoting their healing but we are awakening people to the presence of God, even in their illness.

> **LUKE 10:34** *[A Samaritan] went to [the man who fell into the hands of robbers] and bandaged his wounds, having poured oil and wine on them.*

A duty to care

❦ The announcement of God's presence in suffering and the healing effects of that presence both physically and spiritually comes from the Letter of James. James states that ministers of the church are to attend to the needs of the ill through anointing and prayer. Physically, we are to spread healing oil on the head and hands of the sick. Spiritually, we are to connect the sick to the suffering and death of Jesus. Just as the Father was present to the Son in the midst of his suffering, so is God present to all when they are ill. By anointing them with oil, ministers ask God to send a flood of grace upon the sick to strengthen them in both body and spirit.

> **JAMES 5:14** *Are any among you sick? They should call for the elders of the church and have them pray over them, anointed them with oil in the name of the Lord.*

All in God's hands

❧ The sick person is exhorted by the Christian community to trust that God is at work in his or her life. While our culture sees illness as an unmitigated evil, Anointing the Sick transfigures pain and suffering into a revelation of God's presence. Such trust must be modeled in the life of the minister, however, if it is to be adopted by the sick. Anointing the Sick is a sign that the God who has succored us in our past will continue to guide us into the future.

> **2 MACCABEES 9:22** *I do not despair of my condition, for I have good hope of recovering from my illness.*

Go to all who are sick

❧ If we focus the practice of Anointing the Sick on anyone who may be isolated for any reason from the Christian community, the candidates are many. For example, part of the preparation for surgery should be Anointing the Sick. Those weakened by age and perhaps confined to their homes or to nursing homes may also be anointed regularly, as well as children who are chronically ill. The purpose of this anointing is to prevent the isolation that can accompany illness and to support the sick with the faith of the community, so that anxiety does not interrupt or impede their growth as members of the body of Christ.

> **ACTS 10:38** *[Peter said,] "God anointed Jesus of Nazareth with the Holy Spirit and with power; . . . he went about doing good and healing all who were oppressed by the devil, for God was with him."*

Shared pain

❧ If we ministers share in the joy of others, we should likewise share in their illness. We are a sign that people are not alone in the world; that they are part of a church. By bringing the comfort of the Holy Spirit and the healing presence of God to them, we enable them to share their suffering with the entire community.

> **2 Timothy 1:8** *Do not be ashamed . . . of the testimony about our Lord or of me his prisoner, but join with me in suffering for the gospel, relying on the power of God.*

Go with God

❧ As its name indicates, Anointing the Sick is for those who are ill or infirm. It is not for the dying. The sacrament for the dying is *viaticum*, another name for Eucharist. Meaning "food for the journey," viaticum is the food that sustains us as we cross from life to death to eternal life. Throughout our lives, we remember over and over again the death and resurrection—the Paschal Mystery—of Jesus every time we celebrate Eucharist. Like him, we pass over from life to death to eternal life. The food that nourishes and strengthens us for passing over is the body and blood of Christ.

> **1 Kings 19:7-8** *[The angel said to Elijah,] "Get up and eat, otherwise the journey will be too much for you." He got up, and ate and drank; then he went in the strength of that food forty days and forty nights to Horeb the mount of God.*

On the verge of everlasting life

❧ Before receiving food for the journey, viaticum, the dying person is sprinkled with water to call to mind his or her baptismal sharing in Christ's passion and death, a process of dying and rising that is about to reach a crescendo. Then the person is invited to profess his or her faith for the last time. Thus, for Christians, our last act on this side of the grave is a confession of faith as we, like Jesus, go fearlessly into eternal life. The minister is a sign that God is present even in the act of dying.

> **REVELATION 14:12** *Here is a call for the endurance of the saints, those who keep the commandments of God and hold fast to the faith of Jesus.*

CHAPTER 12

Marriage

The way of life most common in the world is marriage. Two people enter into a communion of life that is so intimate that they partake of the body of one another. Retaining their individuality, they enter into a covenant that mirrors the intimate union of Christ and his body, the church. The couple's act of love-making parallels Eucharist. Just as a married couple give and share their bodies in marriage, so in Eucharist does the whole community share the body and blood of Christ in intimate communion. Through their irrevocable consent, two people vow lifelong fidelity through both good and bad times, through both sickness and health, and promise to love and honor each other. They vow to share the grace of God with each other, even as God shares divine life with them.

The long haul

❦ Marriage is a lifelong process, not a single moment in time. The relationship begins with the first meeting. It progresses as more time is spent together. The two individuals probe the depths of each other and, gradually, come to know the other. At some point in the process, both agree to make the relationship exclusive. Later, they may decide to get engaged, which establishes the ultimate goal of marriage. Finally, along the continuum of this lifelong relationship, they commit themselves to one another permanently, and both agree to foster the growth of the other for the rest of their lives. In this, they are ministers of God's grace—to each other and to the community.

> **1 JOHN 4:16** *We have known and believe the love that God has for us. God is love, and those who abide in love abide in God, and God abides in them.*

Promises, promises

❦ The commitment that each partner in a marriage makes to the other is sealed with a vow. That vow says that—no matter what happens—both parties promise to respect, honor, and be faithful to the other. The vow enables the couple to live freely in their love for one another and in God's love for them. It frames their lives in a unique lifelong relationship. All the Christian minister does is witness those vows on behalf of the entire community.

> **HEBREWS 13:4** *Let marriage be held in honor by all.*

Becoming a family

❦ The basic unit of any society is the family. Besides the mutual growth of the partners, marriage also provides the ideal environment for children. Children are the living results of the love of their parents. And just as they are the fruit of their parents' love, so children share in the depths of that love through the nurturing and care offered them by their parents.

ROMANS 8:15-16 *When we cry, "Abba! Father!" it is that very Spirit bearing witness with our spirit that we are children of God.*

Threefold love

❧ The Greek language has three words for love: *agape*, which designates the love that members of a group or community have for one another; *philos*, which is the love that a brother has for his brother or a sister for her sister; and *eros*, the intimate union of two people in marriage. Through marriage, people pledge a lifetime of all three kinds of love. *Agape* flows from *philos*, which flows from *eros*. And *eros* is made flesh in *philos*, which reaches out in *agape*. The interaction of all three types of love challenges the marriage partners with a lifetime of loving.

1 JOHN 4:21 *The commandment we have from him is this; those who love God must love their brothers and sisters also.*

With this ring

❧ Our culture tends to signify marriage with a ring worn on the left hand of both husband and wife. The circular quality of each ring indicates that the marriage relationship is one of fidelity and unity. During the marriage ceremony, each partner places a ring on the other's finger to represent the gift that each person is. They entrust themselves into the hands of each other and promise to foster both security and freedom in their marriage.

1 MACCABEES 11:9 *Come, let us make a covenant with each other.*

Ministers of the Marriage

🌾 Overemphasis on rings, flowers, clothes, and parties can detract from the primary symbol of marriage—the couple. The bride and groom are the ministers of marriage; the church's minister merely serves to witness the vows they make to each other. The joining of their right hands represents the joining of themselves, their giving of self, and their receiving of the other in freedom. For only in freedom can one person make a gift of self to another. To the other members of the community, the gift of two people in marriage signifies the gift of the bridegroom, Christ, to his bride, the church, and the gift of the church to Christ in a communion of love.

> **GENESIS 2:24** *A man leaves his father and his mother and clings to his wife, and they become one flesh.*

Community commitment

🌾 A wedding ceremony is not merely for the two people entering into marriage, even though they are the focus. Through the marriage rite, the couple invites the rest of the community to share in the couple's love, just as the couple has shared and will share in the community's love. Both those making marriage vows and all those witnessing the vows enter into communion with one another. And, as members of the body of Christ, they give themselves to one another.

> **HEBREWS 13:1** *Let mutual love continue.*

Bound and loose

🌾 Mutual love in marriage does not bind one person to another; it frees both of them to be who they truly are. If marital love becomes constrictive, the life is squeezed out of the marriage. If love frees both parties to develop and become whole, it enhances the marriage relationship. As each partner in a relationship develops his or her individuality, he or she brings new energy to the marriage, which serves to enrich it.

> **1 JOHN 3:16** *We know love by this, that he laid down his life for us—and we ought to lay down our lives for one another.*

Until death sets them free

✿ Death is the ultimate act of freeing a spouse in love. The surviving partner's pain and sadness will eventually be accompanied by the joy of faith that the other is in the bosom of God. Continued communication with the beloved through prayer will free the living spouse to faithfully complete his or her own journey to everlasting life, until the two lovers are once again united in perfect love.

> **REVELATION 19:9** *The angel said to me, "Write this: Blessed are those who are invited to the marriage supper of the Lamb."*

CHAPTER 13

Holy Orders

Ministry of leadership to the Christian community is often sacramentalized into one of three roles. Not to be understood in an exclusive or hierarchical sense, ordained service is manifest in the roles of bishop, priest, and deacon. These ministries differ in their function, but not in terms of one being more important or more powerful than another. These three aspects of ministry are referred to as Holy Orders, but bishops, priests, and deacons become holy not because of their own effort but because the community validates their call from God to be of service to the church. Their primary work as ministers is to gather the community and to orchestrate its worship. While only some Christian ministers receive the formal sacrament of Holy Orders, all ministers share in this ministry.

Called by the community

❦ Holy Orders defines the way ordained ministers live their lives. It continues to be understood and deepened every time a bishop, priest, or deacon leads a community in the celebration of a sacrament or worship service. This ministry is not a one-time-only event. It is a living reality called into existence by the community. The ordained minister proclaims the presence and action of God's grace in the community, and the community reconfirms the minister's call to lead it, along with all its other ministers, in becoming what it already is—the body of Christ.

> **MARK 9:35** *[Jesus] sat down, called the twelve, and said to them, "Whoever wants to be first must be last of all and servant of all."*

Baptised for service

❦ Ordained ministry does not lessen the fact that the primary sacrament of all ministry is Baptism. Holy Orders flows out of the shared baptismal call of all Christians and deepens it. In addition to what is common to all members of the body of Christ, certain people are entrusted with the mission of specific service to the church. To signify the link to Baptism, bishops, priests, and deacons usually wear a white baptismal garment, an alb, when they function in a role of ritual service to the community. (The word *alb* comes from the Latin *albus*, meaning "white.")

> **REVELATION 7:14B** *These are they who have come out of the great ordeal; they have washed their robes and made them white in the blood of the Lamb.*

Servants of servants

Bishops are the successors to the apostles in service to the body of Christ. Jesus chose disciples, followers who would continue his work, and sent them into the world. This is what *apostle* means: "one who is sent." Even though he never met the historical Jesus, Paul called himself an "apostle," because he believed that he had been sent by God to the Gentiles, as those chosen by Jesus had been sent to the Jews. To continue this ministry in the world, the historical apostles appointed others, whom we call bishops, to continue their role of gathering and leading in worship the body of Christ, the church.

> **ROMANS 1:1** *Paul, a servant of Jesus Christ, called to be an apostle, set apart for the gospel of God ....*

Building up the Body of Christ

To fulfill the function of gathering and leading the flock that has been entrusted to a bishop's care, the bishop calls priests and deacons to "holy orders." These ministers share the specific ministry of the bishop and assist in building up the body of Christ, the church. The bishop's function is to teach, sanctify, and guide a diocese or "local church," and the bishop shares the fullness of this ministry with others for the sake of all. Collectively, all bishops, priests, and deacons are first and foremost servants of all the baptized believers.

> **MATTHEW 23:11** *"The greatest among you will be your servant."*

Anointed to serve Christ

Just as in Baptism and Confirmation, anointing with chrism oil in Holy Orders signifies the reception of the gift of the Holy Spirit for the service of all. All Christians, through Baptism and Confirmation, are called to ministry as the grace of the Spirit unfolds throughout their lives. The anointing in Holy Orders commissions its recipients to facilitate the ministry of all believers.

> **PSALM 133:1-2** *How very good and pleasant it is when kindred live together in unity! It is like the precious oil on the head, running down upon the beard, on the bear of Aaron, running down over the collar of his robes.*

God's shepherd

Sometimes called a *crosier*, the pastoral staff carried by bishops is supposed to symbolize a simple shepherd's crook. The bishop carries it as a sign of his function as shepherd of a diocese or "local church." *Pastor* is the Latin word for "shepherd," one who guides and cares for a flock, even to the point of dying for them. The crook of the staff identifies the bishop as one who both sets free the entangled and brings back those who stray. The bishop's main work is to learn to know the members of Christ's body and come to be known by them as one committed to their care.

> **PSALM 80:1** *Give ear, O Shepherd of Israel, you who lead Joseph like a flock! You who are enthroned upon the cherubim, shine forth.*

Encircled in love

A circular band is a sign of eternity: never beginning, never ending, always becoming. In marriage, two people exchange rings as a sign of their lifelong commitment to fidelity. Bishops also wear a ring to represent their eternal commitment of fidelity to the church. The bishop is joined to the church by the solemn promises to serve the Christian community for life; to sustain it and journey with it on the way to salvation; to show kindness and compassion to all its members, especially the poor, strangers, and those in need; to seek out any members who stray and gather them back into the body of Christ; and to pray for all humankind without ceasing.

> **GENESIS 41:42** *Removing his signet ring from his hand, Pharaoh put it on Joseph's hand; he arrayed him in garments of fine linen, and put a gold chain around his neck.*

Feed my lambs

Because bishops cannot minister to every local congregation or parish, they delegate priests to assist them in serving, uniting, and building up the body of Christ. Priests share in the bishop's function as teachers. After reflecting on the word of God, they provide biblical and doctrinal instruction through their preaching. After reflecting on the word of God, they should likewise put into practice what they teach. Then, both as members of the body of Christ and sharing in the bishop's function of teaching, the lives of priests—modeled after that of Jesus—will attract followers to his church through word and action.

> **ROMANS 15:16** *[Grace has been given to me by God] to be a minister of Christ Jesus to the Gentiles in the priestly service of the gospel of God, so that the offering of the Gentiles may be acceptable, sanctified by the Holy Spirit.*

Make us holy, Lord

Priests, like bishops, are commissioned with leading people to holiness. They assist members of the body of Christ in recognizing and naming God's presence in sacramental signs. Although the Spirit works through all members of Christ's body, priests are entrusted in a special way with guiding the manifestations of the Spirit to the service of the common good. Holiness is a community effort, not an individual preoccupation, and priests are supposed to remind everyone of this.

> **HEBREWS 5:1** *Every high priest chosen from among mortals is put in charge of things pertaining to God on their behalf, to offer gifts and sacrifices for sins.*

Pray always

❦ Priests serve the community as leaders of prayer. They guide assemblies through rituals during which people find themselves set free from self-preoccupation to become a unified body, connected with its head, Christ. To lead others into prayer, priests must be persons of prayer themselves. In other words, they practice personally the function they serve publicly, and their public service enhances their private prayer.

> **PHILIPPIANS 4:6** *Do not worry about anything, but in everything by prayer and supplication with thanksgiving let your requests be made known to God.*

Servants of justice

❦ Also sharing in the bishop's role of service to the church are deacons. Their primary responsibility—going back to New Testament times—consists of meeting the charitable and social-justice needs of the body of Christ, such as feeding the hungry, providing housing for the homeless, and welcoming strangers. The very name of the order, *diaconate*, comes from the Greek word *diaconia,* meaning "service." The deacon's function springs primarily from the church's concern for the neediest members of society. The manner in which deacons engage in this work defines their ministry.

MATTHEW 25:40 *"The king will [say], 'Truly I tell you, just as you did it to one of the least of these who are members of my family, you did it to me.'"*

Bringing the gospel to life

✼ During their ordination, deacons are presented a *Book of Gospels* to signify their role of sharing in the bishop's function as teacher. Deacons are called to teach what the church believes and to practice what they teach through their social service to the community. The teaching ministry of deacons springs from their connection to the altar as liturgical assistants of the bishop and priests. Drawing their strength from the Holy Spirit, those in the order of deacons bring the word of God they preach to those whom they serve socially. Thus is the gospel made manifest in the ministry of the deacon.

MARK 8:35 *"Those who want to save their life will lose it, and those who lose their life for my sake, and for the sake of the gospel, will save it."*

CHAPTER 14

Ministers & Ministry

B esides those who are specifically ordained to serve the community through Holy Orders, there are countless others whose baptismal grace unfolds in ministry to the members of the body of Christ and to the world. In their collective effort to proclaim, serve, and further realize the always-in-the-process-of-becoming reign of God, all of these other ministers experience their callings as ones that flow from the Spirit's gifts and match the unique personality of each individual.

Proclaimers of the Word

❧ The lector's, or Scripture reader's, function is to read the word of God in the assembly of believers. But lectors do more than read; they interpret what they proclaim after careful study and reflection on the biblical passages. As the members of the body of Christ hear the word of God delivered to them through a lector, they are fed with a faith that is rooted in the Scriptures. Through their manner of proclamation, lectors demonstrate that they have accepted the Good News themselves in obedience to the Holy Spirit, who inspired the Word and continues to inspire its proclaimers.

> **1 Timothy 4:6** *If you put these instructions before the brothers and sisters, you will be a good servant of Christ Jesus, nourished on the words of the faith and of the sound teaching that you have followed.*

Ministers at the Lord's table

❧ The Christian community is served the body and blood of Christ primarily through the hands of those chosen for ordained ministry: bishops, priests, and deacons. But because of the gratifying number of members of most congregations, eucharistic ministers are usually needed to facilitate sharing from the Lord's table. From the table at which they themselves are nourished, they help share the body and blood of Christ with their sisters and brothers with whom they form the living body of Christ. By also carrying the Eucharist to the sick and home-bound, these ministers of care demonstrate the community's love for its absent members.

> **John 12:26** *"Whoever serves me must follow me, and where I am, there will my servant be also. Whoever serves me, the Father will honor."*

At the service of others

Those who carry the cross, candles, and incense; hold the sacred books; and handle other articles used in liturgical celebration are altar servers. In the name of the entire community, altar servers assist the leaders of the assembly. They usually wear a white garment to signify that their service flows from their Baptism. There ministry is a reminder that every member of the Christian community has the obligation to serve all the other members of the body of Christ.

> **Luke 22:27** *[Jesus asked his disciples,] "Who is greater, the one who is at the table or the one who serves? Is it not the one at the table? But I am among you as one who serves."*

Welcome the stranger

Ushers facilitate the gathering of the members of the Christian community by offering words of welcome as people arrive for liturgy, meetings, or special events. They also are the ones who take up collections, see to people's special needs, and handle any problems that arise. When ushers serve the community well, the body of Christ is already manifest in the unity of welcoming and hospitality, before a word of formal worship is spoken or a hymn of praise is sung.

> **Hebrews 13:2** *Do not neglect to show hospitality to strangers, for by doing that some have entertained angels without knowing it.*

Sing a new song

One of the ways we give glory to God is through song. Musicians assist the Christian community by composing, arranging, and directing our sung prayer. Through their ministry, musicians also set the tone for our celebrations—whether they are to be quiet and contemplative or raucous and soulful. Musicians use their gifts to heighten our awareness of God's presence and help harmonize our thanksgiving.

> **1 CHRONICLES 15:28** *All of Israel brought up the ark of the covenant of the LORD with shouting, to the sound of the horn, trumpets, and cymbals, and made loud music on harps and lyres.*

A voice for the people

Sometimes called a song leader or leader of song, a cantor is entrusted with the function of leading the members of the body of Christ in praise, especially the responsorial singing of psalms and other songs and hymns. This ministry is not one for display or artistry for itself, but one in which one person's ability to sing is offered to the whole community as a gift to be shared. Through the singing gifts of cantors, the many voices of the assembly are united into one harmonious voice of praise.

> **COLOSSIANS 3:16** *Let the word of Christ dwell in you richly; teach and admonish one another in all wisdom; and with gratitude in your hearts sing psalms, hymns, and spiritual songs to God.*

All together now

The ministry of the choir is not performance for, but service to, the community. The unity of the choir mirrors the unity of the whole body of Christ. The harmonious voices of the various members of the choir utilize their individual gifts for the good of the whole. The choir becomes a miniature picture of the church, working together to praise the Lord.

SIRACH 40:20 *Wine and music gladden the heart, but the love of friends is better than either.*

The People of God assembled

❧ The most important ministry of all is that of the assembly. It is a ministry to which we all belong. In the assembly, members of the body of Christ gather to manifest to one another who we already are by the fact of our common Baptism. Each member of the assembly facilitates the ministry of all others through the process of gathering, welcoming, processing, praying, and singing. In a word, members of the assembly have a ministry of presence to one another. Through this presence, we recognize the need to call upon those given the gifts to lead the assembly in its worship and song. Thus, all ministry flows from and back to the body of Christ.

1 TIMOTHY 1:2 *Grace, mercy, and peace from God the Father and Christ Jesus our Lord.*

The Alpha and the Omega

❧ Ministry is service to the members of the body of Christ and to the world. Each person, from bishops to the members of the assembly, manifests a gift for service that is given by the Spirit and is vital to the building of a unified Christian community. Forever connected through Baptism, we ministers provide various types of service in our efforts to reveal to one another that the Christ we share from the Lord's table is the same Christ who gathers around that table. He is both the beginning and the end—the *alpha* and the *omega*—of Christian service.

> **REVELATION 19:10** *"I am a fellow servant with you and your comrades who hold the testimony of Jesus. Worship God. For the testimony of Jesus is the spirit of prophecy."*

The Christian's mission

❧ Ministry within the body of Christ inexorably leads to mission outside the body. After gathering around the table of the Lord in worship, Christian ministers are sent forth in service to the world. We offer the world hope, comfort, and encouragement. Being sent out provides us with the opportunity to live the faith we celebrate within our local gatherings amidst the rest of the people of the world. Yet even as we fulfill our mission, we are called back to intensify our identity and become again who we already are—the body of Christ.

> **REVELATION 2:19** *"I know your works—your love, faith, service, and patient endurance. I know that your last works are greater than the first."*

Salvation is ours

❧ In our awareness that the grace we receive from God is simultaneously flowing inward and outward, we recognize a moment of salvation. The way to become fully human is to be filled with divine grace. And the way to become divine is to be fully human. The more we give away the grace that unites us, the more we receive and experience unity. In other words, there is more grace when it is given away than when it is kept. This paradox of grace is the foundation for ministry. In the act of our giving and receiving service, God saves us all.

> **1 PETER 1:10** *Concerning this salvation, the prophets who prophesied of the grace that was to be yours made careful search and inquiry.*

With open hearts

❧ The movement of grace in ministry fosters greater and greater openness, not only of people to one another but of people to God. As the spiral of openness swings in an ever-widening coil, it gathers into one body those whom God has graced at ever-deepening levels of their humanity. Openness serves its own purpose of weaving together the threads of the tapestry that reveal who the community of service is always becoming—the body of Christ.

> **HEBREWS 5:8-9** *Although he was a Son, [Jesus] learned obedience through what he suffered; and having been made perfect, he became the source of eternal salvation for all who obey him.*

Animate the world

❧ The members of the body of Christ in service to one another— that is, all ministers—animate the world. We give it life through our turning—our conversion—toward one another. Through our ministry, grace is set free and the Spirit of God is let loose to draw all of creation to openness. God initiates the offer, but it requires our free response. We serve others by awakening them to the realization that God is already present in their lives. They go away knowing that they have found in us what they have sought for so long for themselves.

> **MARK 10:43** *"Whoever wishes to become great among you must be your servant."*

CHAPTER 15

Images of Church

Every person who belongs to the body of Christ has an image of church, a fundamental way of thinking about the Christian community. Sometimes called "models" or "paradigms," images of church enable us to talk about the reality of a group of individuals who, for whatever reasons, freely join together to participate in religiously-motivated activities, especially worship. The primary image of church used in this book has been the Pauline model of the body of Christ, but this is not the only way of organizing our thoughts concerning what the community of believers is and what it can be. We employ many different images or metaphors to express what we mean by "church."

Upon this rock: teach, sanctify, govern

❦ One way to think about the church is as a public organization or institution, insofar as its members gather in one place and are arranged in some type of order. The primary ministry of the institution is to teach, sanctify, and govern the membership. When the institution teaches, it insists that its teaching ought to be believed by all its members. When it sanctifies, it exhorts its membership not only to follow certain rules but to grow in cooperation with God's grace. It governs by some type of hierarchy, elected or appointed, which is entrusted with the duty of making decisions on behalf of the membership. The institutional church provides links to the past and provides a sense of corporate identity to its members.

1 PETER 2:13 *For the Lord's sake accept the authority of every human institution.*

Body of Christ: all parts of the whole

❦ The image of the church as the body of Christ is an organic model that approaches the assembly of believers from the perspectives of mutual union, concern, and dependence. The head of the body is Christ, and the enlivening principle is the Holy Spirit, who distributes gifts to every individual member for the common good. When the individual members gather, they make partially visible the body of Christ. One is initiated forever into this body through Baptism, but the complete body remains only partially visible because some members have died and some have not yet been born. Nevertheless, the body of believers is bound together through its faith, worship, and fellowship, which are inspired by the Spirit.

ROMANS 12:5 *We, who are many, are one body in Christ, and individually we are members one of another.*

Pilgrim people: journeying toward God

❧ We are journeying through time; thus, we are called a pilgrim people. This image has its earliest roots in the story of Abraham and Sarah, who left their native land and traveled to a new place as God directed them. Abraham was not sure where he was going, but he went in the hope that God would not disappoint or frustrate him. Where Abraham and Sarah left off, Moses and Zipporah took up by leading God's people on a journey to the promised land. Following Christ's death and resurrection, Christians now follow the way of the cross toward God.

> **HEBREWS 11:8** *By faith Abraham obeyed when he was called to set out for a place that he was to receive as an inheritance; and he set out, not knowing where he was going.*

Sacrament: a sign of Christ

❧ A sacrament is an action by a community of believers who make visible God's invisible offer of grace. The church has always considered itself a sign of God's saving activity in the world. This activity, which seeks expression through the lives of the Christian people, impels us to demonstrate the church's essence as a sign of Christ. Thus, the church shares God's grace with its own members who, in turn, scatter it into the world.

> **JOHN 6:14** *When the people saw the sign that [Jesus] had done, they began to say, "This is indeed the prophet who is to come into the world."*

Herald: spreading the Good News

✝ The mission of the church is to proclaim the word it has heard. Thus, its membership becomes simultaneously hearers and heralds of the word. Faith is a response to that word and is demonstrated by all of us gathering to be commissioned to spread the Good News throughout the world. Such preaching finds its roots in Jesus and the prophets, who still call people to take advantage of the salvation God offers here and now. When the church is a herald, the word of God becomes an incarnational event.

> **2 TIMOTHY 1:11** *For this gospel I was appointed a herald and an apostle and a teacher.*

Servant: putting God's mercy to work

✝ The servant church reaches outward to others and offers words of comfort or encouragement. It is willing to listen to those in need, and it offers material help to the poor, homeless, or sick and spiritual support to the lonely, ignorant, or frightened. In this understanding of church, the minister serves the Christian community by leading it deeper and deeper into its role of meeting the needs of the world.

> **REVELATION 19:10** *I am a fellow servant with you and your comrades who hold the testimony of Jesus. Worship God!*

Vine and branches: continuing to grow

✝ The flow of life in a grape arbor works well as a model of the church. Last year's growth of branches is pruned back to facilitate new growth and a fruitful harvest. The old growth vine remains firmly rooted in the earth, from which it draws water and minerals to sustain its life. Sending out new branches each year, the vine maintains the life of the branches. The community of believers, the body of Christ, serves as the vine, bringing the life of Christ to the world. The mission of the minister is to ensure that the branches remain connected to the vine, so that they can continue to grow.

> **JOHN 15:5** *"I am the vine, you are the branches. Those who abide in me and I in them bear much fruit, because apart from me you can do nothing."*

Bride: promised to Christ

The church can be understood as the bride of Christ. Using the wedding metaphor, the bride—the community of believers—is joined to the groom—Christ—through baptismal promises. Just as husband and wife pledge a lifetime of nourishment and growth to one another, so the members of the church promise to bring one another to their fullest potential. The intimacy that manifests the union of man and woman becomes a model of how closely united the church, the bride, is to Christ, her husband. It is through the lifetime development of faith that the members of the Christian community are led to their final union with Christ by their ministers.

> **REVELATION 19:7** *Let us rejoice and exult and give [God] the glory, for the marriage of the Lamb has come, and his bride has made herself ready.*

Living stones: built to last

While we do not usually think of stones as being alive, they nevertheless can serve as a good model of the church. Each member is like a stone that is used in constructing a magnificent building. The stone is prepared by a cutter, who shapes it for its place in the whole structure. No one stone is more important than any other. From the individual stones, a building rises. From the individual members of the church, a community of believers is built and is constantly in the process of being rebuilt through the addition of new members. Thus, the living stones of the church continue to become even more a building meant to last.

1 PETER 2:5 *Like living stones, let yourselves be built into a spiritual house, to be a holy priesthood, to offer spiritual sacrifices acceptable to God through Jesus Christ.*

Banquet table: no one goes hungry

❦ The church is like a large round table around which all the members sit. The round table indicates the equality of all who are gathered. Those who serve are no less or more important than those who eat because each has a place at the table. The banquet is shared by all. Every person is filled from the feast spread on the table—even the hungriest and those with nothing to share except themselves. The choice wine and food give but a taste of the fullness to be revealed in God's reign.

ACTS 2:42 *They devoted themselves to the apostles' teaching and fellowship, to the breaking of bread and the prayers.*

CHAPTER 16

The Church Building

We Christian ministers serve the members of our congregations in the church building, a sacred space set aside for worship. From the worship that takes place in that space flows the service that the congregation enacts—both individually and collectively—in the world. Service to the world then brings the members back to the church building—both to celebrate what God has done through us and to share our failures and defeats with one another. The church building is not the church, but it is the place where church is formed and nourished.

Baptismal font: immersed in new life

❦ The baptismal font, found near the door of most church buildings, is the place of sacramental initiation into the body of Christ. The font is at the door to remind all who pass by that it is through water that our old life ends and our new life begins. Filled or flowing with water, the essence of life, the font beckons all members of the church to remember that Baptism is the source for all ministry. All who are baptized are called to serve one another, to build up the church, to be the presence of Christ in the world today.

> JOEL 3:18 *In that day the mountains shall drip sweet wine, the hills shall flow with milk, and all the stream beds of Judah shall flow with water; a fountain shall come forth from the house of the LORD.*

Easter Candle: the light of Christ

❦ Standing near the baptismal font is the Easter Candle, a large pillar of wax lit during the Easter Vigil, proclaimed to be "Christ our light" and the column of fire that leads us on our pilgrimage of faith. The newly baptized receive a small candle lit from the Easter Candle to signify that they have been raised to new life with the risen Christ through the watery tomb/womb of Baptism. Not only are they to walk in the light of Christ, but they are to spread it throughout the world. The God who is pure light calls all followers of Jesus to the ministry of scattering the darkness of homelessness, poverty, and sickness with the baptismal light of the Son.

> JOHN 9:5 *"As long as I am in the world, I am the light of the world."*

Chrism oil: anointed ones

✢ In many new churches, we find a container housing three vials of oil displayed near the baptismal font. The container, called an ambry, is a box for storing the oils used in worship services. One of these oils, *chrism*, is used to anoint people in Baptism, Confirmation, and Holy Orders. It is also used to bless the altar when a new church building is dedicated, symbolizing that all of God's people are to be "other Christs" in service to one another. In a sense, then, all of us are anointed.

> **HEBREWS 1:9** *God, your God, has anointed you with the oil of gladness beyond your companions.*

Oil of catechumens: strengthened in faith

✢ The second oil found in the ambry is named *catechumens* because it is used to strengthen those preparing to declare their faith publicly through Baptism. Catechumens are in the process of being catechized or taught the fundamentals of the Christian faith. The anointing of catechumens preserves them in their developing faith. Faith is a way of life, and catechumens need the help of those who have already been initiated to sustain their journey to the baptismal font. When they are anointed with the oil of catechumens, they are anointed with the strength of the community itself.

> **PSALM 23:5** *You prepare a table before me in the presence of my enemies; you anoint my head with oil; my cup overflows.*

Oil of the sick: healing touch

✢ The third oil in the ambry is the oil of the sick. We all use oil-based salves to ease sore muscles, to bring warmth to aching joints, to soften dry skin. Following Jesus' example, ministers heal—sometimes by anointing the ill or infirm with the oil of the sick, sometimes by anointing the sick with words of comfort, sometimes by merely being present and offering a gentle touch to another's hand. Anointing the sick with oil declares that God is working to effect a cure of whatever is keeping a person from full participation in the community of faith.

> **JAMES 5:14** *Are any among you sick? They should call for the elders of the church and have them pray over them, anointing them with oil in the name of the LORD.*

Altar: seated at the Lord's table

In virtually every church, there is an altar. It is often a simple rectangular table, whose purpose is to serve the meal of the Eucharist. As we do in our homes, we gather in church around this table, upon which has been placed the one who was sacrificed for our lives. When we break bread and share wine around the Lord's table, we as a community become visibly who we already are: the body of Christ. The food and drink we consume signifies that we are willing to sacrifice ourselves for one another through our ministry to one another.

> **MATTHEW 23:19** *"Which is greater, the gift or the altar that makes the gift sacred?"*

Eucharist: life-giving banquet

Once a new altar has been sprinkled with water, anointed with chrism oil, and clothed in white during its dedication, its initiation is completed with the first meal served upon it. In other words, it truly becomes what it signifies—the table from which the members of Christ's body are nourished, the table upon which is spread the life-giving banquet. Those members of the community who are gathered around the altar join themselves together in a unity whose bonds are nothing other than God's grace. To this table all will return repeatedly to become again and again the body of Christ.

> **MATTHEW 5:23-24** *When you are offering your gift at the altar, if you remember that you brother or sister has something against you, leave your gift there before the altar and go; first be reconciled to your brother or sister, and then come and offer your gift.*

Ambo: a table for the word

❦ The word of God is usually proclaimed from the lectern, podium, pulpit, or ambo—a reading desk or table for the word. Just as the altar serves as the table where the feast of bread and wine is spread, so is the ambo the place where God's word is proclaimed and broken open by ministers of the community. For Christians to remain spiritually alive, we need the sustenance that come from the word as it is offered to us from the ambo. Those who serve the community as lectors, deacons, priests, and preachers are entrusted with this ministry of the word.

> **2 TIMOTHY 3:16** *All scripture is inspired by God and is useful for teaching, for reproof, for correction, and for training in righteousness.*

Book: bound by God's word

❦ The word of God is represented by a book, called the Bible. Many churches employ other books to signify God's word. A *Lectionary* contains a series of Scripture passages that are proclaimed on designated days. The *Book of Gospels,* as its name implies, contains the selections to be read on specific days. The Christian community does not honor the book—no matter which one is used. We honor the word of God that the book signifies. The care employed in handling the book, the manner in which it may be carried in procession and placed on the ambo, the reverence shown in opening and closing it—these, too, are teachings heard by the community of believers.

> **REVELATION 5:7** *[The Lamb] went and took the scroll from the right hand of the one who was seated on the throne.*

Presider's chair: designated seating

🎋 In most families, the father and the mother have a special place at table. In fact, most of us have a tendency to sit in the same chair—in the kitchen or dining room when we eat, in the living or family room when we relax, in a classroom or office when we study or work. These special chairs give each of us a sense of belonging, of having our own space, of enjoying the comfort of not having to make a decision about where to sit every time we come into a room. Thus, the minister who leads prayer in a church building usually stands in front of and sits in a special chair, which indicates that he or she is the presider or organizer of the liturgical celebration.

> **2 KINGS 4:10** *[The Shunemite woman said to her husband,] "Let us make a small roof chamber with walls, and put there for [Elisha] a bed, a table, a chair, and a lamp, so that he can stay there whenever he comes to us."*

Pews: close contact

🎋 When people sit in a pew, they have a tendency to stay at either end, where at least one side fosters security. Only reluctantly will they move to the center. Pews put us in close contact with other worshipers with whom we share hymnals, touch knees, or rub shoulders as we slip in and out of the space. While chairs encourage personal identity, pews enable a communal identity to emerge.

> **1 Samuel 4:13** *Eli was sitting upon his seat by the road watching, for his heart trembled for the ark of God.*

Reconciliation room: where mercy resides

The "reconciliation room" in a church can be a small room or office furnished with comfortable chairs, a back pew, or a designated space in the sanctuary. The space is not as important as the purpose. The people we serve go to that place seeking reconciliation with others and with God. Because it is in this place that we came face-to-face with mercy flowing from God to all of us and from all of us to one another, the contours of the reconciliation room can become etched in our minds.

> **Colossians 1:20** *Through [Christ] God was pleased to reconcile to himself all things, whether on earth or in heaven, by making peace through the blood of his cross.*

Cross: victory in defeat

Prominently located in most Christian churches is a cross. In the ancient world the cross was a sign of defeat. The man (women were stoned to death, not crucified) nailed to its wood was considered cursed by God. One lesson the cross of Jesus teaches is that victory is achieved exactly where most people would not even think to look. God is not found in a warrior-king messiah, but in a crucified one. God is not found on a lofty, heavenly throne, but nailed to a piece of wood. God is not found only in life, but also in death. God is discovered exactly where people presume that God cannot be found. In other words, the cross connects our divided world. It brings heaven and earth together in one grand scheme of reconciliation and declares that God is present in life and death, in joy and pain, in happiness and suffering. All human opposites are united by the cross.

> **GALATIANS 6:14** *May I never boast of anything except the cross of our Lord Jesus Christ, by which the world has been crucified to me, and I to the world.*

Reservation chapel: community storehouse

❦ Many churches have a room or alcove called the "reservation" chapel or altar in which is kept the bread that remains after the Eucharist has been celebrated. It is often from the reservation chapel that ministers of care carry the eucharistic bread to the sick to show them that they remain members of Christ's body. The dying receive the bread as *viaticum*—"food for their journey" through death to eternal life. Thus, the Eucharist is reserved primarily to keep the community united and included around the Lord's table.

> **2 CHRONICLES 5:7** *The priests brought the ark of the covenant of the LORD to its place, in the inner sanctuary of the house, in the most holy place, underneath the wings of the cherubim.*

Tabernacle: remember our covenant

❦ The tabernacle containing the reserved Eucharist evokes the ark of the covenant, the box containing the tablets of the law carried by the Israelites through their long desert journey and, finally, installed in the Holy of Holies in the temple in Jerusalem. Like the ark, the tabernacle signifies God's covenant with us and presence with us in the person of Jesus Christ. Through his incarnation, Jesus revealed that every human being is a sign of God's presence. In a way, every human being is an ark or a tabernacle. Ministers are responsible for awakening people to this realization.

1 Chronicles 15:28 *All Israel brought up the ark of the covenant of the Lord with shouting, to the sound of the horn, trumpets, and cymbals, and made loud music on harps and lyres.*

Kneelers: an aid for adoration

Another use of the reservation chapel is for adoration. Here people kneel or sit in quiet, private prayer. The adoration of Christ present as Eucharist flows from the community's celebration of itself as the body of Christ. In other words, it is the activity of Eucharist—eating and drinking at the Lord's table, recognizing Christ in one another, and becoming the body of Christ—that leads to adoration. The Christ we adore as we kneel before the reserved Eucharist in the tabernacle is the same Christ we recognize in one another.

Exodus 40:34 *The cloud covered the tent of meeting, and the glory of the Lord filled the tabernacle.*

Real Presence: Christ be with you

Under the form of bread, Christ is really present in the tabernacle. Notice that it is not the historical Jesus in the form of a 30-year-old Jewish man who is present, but rather it is the Christ of faith who is recognized only by those who believe. We cannot separate the real presence of Christ in Eucharist from the real presence of Christ in the members of his body, the church. These are not two presences but rather one activated by the other. Without the members of the body of Christ really present to one another, we cannot celebrate Eucharist. And without celebrating Eucharist, we cannot recognize in one another the real Christ, whose presence we make visible.

MATTHEW 18:20 *"Where two or three are gathered in my name, I am there among them."*

Church building: the people's house

❦ The church building is a house for the church—the people of God who form it and are formed by it. The building and its appointments must possess integrity, a sense of wholeness that is reflected in the community's truthfulness about itself. And the church members' authenticity should be reflected in the honesty of the building. This means that churches are not built and then congregations fitted into them, nor are congregations formed and then churches built to accommodate them. Both the meeting place for the assembly and the community itself are involved in a process of change, a process of always becoming Christ's presence in the world.

> **COLOSSIANS 1:24** *I am now rejoicing in my sufferings for your sake, and in my flesh I am completing what is lacking in Christ's afflictions for the sake of his body, that is, the church.*

Environment: true to its purpose

❦ The basic furnishings of a place for worship must be authentic. The font, altar, ambo, chair, pews, reservation chapel, and reconciliation room should exude genuineness, signifying each one's importance. Water must be plentiful in the font. The altar's shape and size should itself invite the assembly to approach the Lord's table. The ambo should enhance the word, the presider's chair signify trustworthiness, the pews foster community, the reconciliation room enable penitents to feel God's forgiveness.

> **ROMANS 12:9** *Let love be genuine; hate what is evil, hold fast to what is good ....*

Church members: a faithful people

❦ The gathering place for the members of the church represents the faith of the people. The building is their faith incarnate both in the body of Christ they manifest and in the stone, brick, and wood of the structure that houses them. Thus, the faith of a people is seen in the church structures they build. In Europe, for example, we can still see the churches and cathedrals the faithful built that have endured for five hundred years or more. It took generations to finish those huge buildings, but a walk through one is a journey into the faith of those who worshipped in them. Fidelity is timeless and is always in the process of incarnation.

> **SIRACH 1:27** *The fear of the LORD is wisdom and discipline, fidelity and humility are his delight.*

CHAPTER 17

The Home Church

Like the church building in which the members of a community meet to worship God, the home is a sacred place in which members of a family worship together. While a family's worship differs in ritual and form, the home is nevertheless a holy place, a "domestic church." In fact, from the worship in homes flows the worship that takes place in the church building. Those who minister to an assembly of believers should not only foster worship in the home but draw upon the holiness of the home for prayer and song in the midst of the weekly gathering of households that takes place in church.

Cleansed and renewed

❦ Washing is an important action in any home. Daily, we wash away our old selves and emerge clean and new. From the washing we do in our homes, we learn about the cleansing that takes place in church.

> **EPHESIANS 5:25-26** *Christ loved the church and gave himself up for her, in order to make her holy by cleansing her with the washing of water by the word.*

Drawn to the light

❦ We use candles on the dining room tables of our homes for special meals to highlight the dinner's solemnity. Candlelight sets a mood that facilitates sharing and romance. If we want to provide a pleasant smell, scented candles waft vanilla, cranberry, pine, and other aromas throughout our homes. When the electricity goes out during the night, the first thing we scramble for is a match to light a candle so that we can see in the dark. A candle burning in a darkened room draws people toward itself, much like the Easter candle in the church—the sign of the risen Christ—draws us into his light.

> **2 PETER 1:19** *So we have the prophetic message more fully confirmed. You will do well to be attentive to this as to a lamp shining in a dark place, until the day dawns and the morning star rises in your hearts.*

Soothing and nourishing oils

❦ Used to lubricate both machines and people, various types of oils, much like the oils used in anointing during sacramental celebrations, can be found in most homes. A drop of "3-in-one" oil helps keep sewing machines, fans, mixers, and other motorized appliances running smoothly. If we have a sore or strained muscle, we rub in an ointment to generate heat and ease the pain. And in the kitchen we coat, fry, boil, and mix our food with aromatic oils from around the world. The healing oils we use at home are mirrored in the strengthening oils we use in church.

2 THESSALONIANS 2:17 *Comfort your hearts and strengthen them in every good work and word.*

Family gathering

One of the most sacred items in our homes is our dining room table. It was usually chosen with great care and after much deliberation. Gathered around this table, members of a family share the food of their lives. It may also be the place where homework is finished, bills paid, and board games played. The table gets its identity from the family members who seat themselves around it, and if it has been a part of many generations it bears the scratches and dents of the past. It is an altar upon which the members of a family place their joys and sorrows, their brokenness and wholeness, and their pasts, presents, and futures.

LUKE 7:36 *One of the Pharisees asked Jesus to eat with him, and he went into the Pharisee's house and took his place at the table.*

At home with God's word

The coffee table, bookshelf, or table next to a favorite reading chair serves as the place where the Bible is located in our homes. We open and read from it privately as part of our daily devotion. We may read some of its stories to our children before they go to bed at night. Some people find it a rich source for prayer and meditation. The Bible in our home reinforces the same word of God we hear in our churches.

1 Timothy 4:13 *Give attention to the public reading of scripture, to exhorting, to teaching.*

Reconciling differences

❦ Reconciliation can take place in any room in our home, but it will most likely be enacted privately. Husband and wife will work out their differences in their bedroom. Parents will assist children in the process of forgiving one another in the kitchen or den. And, until they can cool down and forgive, children are often sent to their rooms. Peacemaking is an ongoing activity in any household. All of the forgiving that we have done at home is then brought to church, where we acknowledge that God forgives us to the same degree that we have been able to forgive one another.

Daniel 9:9 *To the Lord our God belong mercy and forgiveness.*

Household cross

❦ In almost every Christian home there is at least one cross or crucifix on the wall. The cross with intertwined rings on it may have been a wedding gift. If it has "25" or "50" on it, it most likely was a wedding anniversary commemoration. A narrow silver cross with a corpus on it may have rested on the casket of a deceased relative and is now kept in memory of him or her. A wooden cross with a plaster corpus may have been given on the day one was accepted into the catechumenate or elected to share in the Easter sacraments. The crosses in our homes are signs of the Christian faith we share together as a family, the same faith we later bring to church, where— under one large cross—we share it with other families.

Mark 15:20 *After mocking [Jesus], they stripped him of the purple cloak and put his own clothes on him. Then they led him out to crucify him.*

CHAPTER 18

Sunday

We Christian ministers are most visible on Sundays, when we are engaged in teaching and prayer with others. The "day of rest" for most people often becomes the most intense workday for ministers. Sunday duties present the biggest challenge to those who serve congregations. We cannot share the deeper importance or meaning of the Sabbath with others if we have not incorporated it into our own lives. Sunday is not merely several hours of worship on the weekend; it is a whole attitude of recognizing the sacredness of our entire week.

Easter Sunday

✤ Sunday derives its importance for Christians as the day of Christ's resurrection. Every Sunday is a miniature Easter Sunday—a "little Easter"—when the whole church remembers that God did not abandon Jesus but rather raised him from the dead. Easter Sunday contains the heart, the core, the center of fragile Christian faith. It is the pivot point upon which all forms of Christianity turn. Without Easter there is no Christian faith. Without Easter, there would be no gospels, no letters of Paul, no Book of Revelation. Easter is so full of meaning that it takes all other Sundays of the year to unpack it. And every one of those fifty-one Sundays looks back to Easter for its inspiration.

> **JOHN 20:1** *Early on the first day of the week, while it was still dark, Mary Magdalene came to the tomb and saw that the stone had been removed from the tomb.*

Pentecost

✤ Christians gather for worship on Sunday not only because that is the day when God raised Jesus from the dead but because it is also the day when God gave the church the gift of the Spirit. Only the evangelist Luke, in the Acts of the Apostles, recounts how 50 days after Easter God's Spirit descended as tongues of fire that gave the timid disciples the ability to speak and understand various languages. The gifts of the Spirit even today continue to create order from chaos, unity from diversity, and life from death. Christians gather on Sunday so that the Spirit can weave us into a tapestry of salvation for ourselves and our world.

> **TOBIT 2:1** *I [Tobit] returned home, and my wife Anna and my son Tobias were restored to me. At our festival of Pentecost, which is the sacred festival of weeks, a good dinner was prepared for me and I reclined to eat.*

First day

Sunday is often referred to as "the first day of the week," because on that day, when the Jewish Sabbath was over, the dead Jesus was first encountered as alive by the disciples, led by Mary Magdalene. They also experienced the risen Christ through their gatherings, prayers, and the breaking of bread, just as we do today. So the early Christians decided that Sunday was the appropriate day for their worship, and thus the first day of the week was set aside to celebrate the "firstborn of the dead" and to renew our hope that the new life that God gave to Christ will be given to all.

> **ACTS 20:7** *On the first day of the week, when we met to break bread, Paul was holding a discussion . . . ; since he intended to leave the next day, he continued speaking until midnight.*

Eighth day

Besides being called the first day of the week, Sunday is sometimes called "the eighth day." In the ancient world, zero had not yet been invented; it was not a concept. Thus, when people counted, they began with one. We'd say that seven days have elapsed from one Sunday to the next, but they'd count eight. Thus, from a Jewish point of view, a perfect or complete week consisted of eight days. Also referred to as "the octave," worshipping on Sunday became an appropriate way to indicate Christ's resurrection.

> **NEHEMIAH 8:18** *Day by day, from the first day to the last day, [Ezra] read from the book of the law of God. They kept the festival [of booths] seven days' and on the eighth day there was a solemn assembly.*

New creation

❦ When Jesus was raised from the dead, God did something new—re-creating not only all humankind but the whole earth as well. Thus, Sunday is often referred to as "the day of new creation." For on Sunday we recall the resurrection of Jesus and realize that even now God is in the process of re-creating us and preparing us for our own resurrection from the dead.

> **2 CORINTHIANS 5:17** *If anyone is in Christ, there is a new creation: everything old has passed away; see, everything has become new!*

Lord's Day

❦ For the early Christians, Sunday's purpose was to set aside time for praise and thanksgiving to God for the resurrection of Christ, the gift of the Holy Spirit, and the revelation of the Father as a God who is deeply in love with and shares the life of grace with all of creation. Praise and thanksgiving were offered through common prayer and meal-sharing, as these brought together people who acknowledged Jesus Christ as Lord. Thus, it became "the Lord's Day."

> **REVELATION 1:10** *I was in the spirit on the Lord's day, and I heard behind me a loud voice like a trumpet ....*

Sunday

❦ No matter what we call it—little Easter, Pentecost, the first day or the eighth day, the day of new creation, or the Lord's Day—Sunday is for regeneration, renewal, recuperation, redirection. Momentarily, it lifts us out of our dailiness and offers a respite so that we can gather with other Christians for worship, join family members to eat, and stand back and look at the bigger picture of the world instead of our little corner of it. We Christian ministers, whose responsibility it is to guide others in the observance of Sunday, must check ourselves to be sure that in so doing we have not led ourselves out of it.

> **MARK 16:2** *When the Sabbath was over, Mary Magdalene and Mary the mother of James, and Salome bought spices, so that they might go and anoint [Jesus].*

CHAPTER 19

God of Resurrection

Any attempt to talk about God ultimately ends in futility. If we could capture God in words, then by definition God would no longer be God. So, in our feeble efforts we ministers usually speak about what God is not, thinking that will satisfy both others and ourselves. As we know, however, we cannot quench the human desire to know God. And while we may at times capture a microscopic glimpse of God, no words are adequate for sharing that experience with others. In the end, we have to be content with saying that silence best defines God. And when we have been silent and said nothing, then we have said it all.

God of Moses

❧ The God who appeared to Moses in a burning bush was revealed as the same God of the patriarchs and matriarchs—Abraham and Sarah, Isaac and Rebecca, and Jacob and Rachel. But Moses received a further revelation of God's identity: "I am who I am" or simply "I am." This same God who called Abraham and Sarah to begin their nation-founding pilgrimage is nothing less than the totality of being. It is this reality who led the Hebrews out of Egypt and will lead all of us to the promised land.

> **EXODUS 3:14** *God said to Moses, "I AM WHO I AM." he said further, "Thus you shall say to the Israelites, 'I AM has sent me to you.'"*

God of Elijah

❧ Elijah, one of the greatest prophets, has no biblical book bearing his name, but that does not diminish his importance in revealing the true nature of God. God was experienced by Elijah in the one place he didn't expect. After looking for God in the power of wind, earthquake, and fire, Elijah finally recognized the Lord in "the sound of sheer silence."

> **1 KINGS 19:11-12** *The LORD was not in the wind; and after the wind an earthquake, but the LORD was not in the earthquake; and after the earthquake a fire, but the LORD was not in the fire; and after the fire a sound of sheer silence.*

God of Jesus

❧ According to Mark's account of the transfiguration, both Moses and Elijah appear and speak with Jesus. This is meant to symbolize that Jesus' God is the same Lord whom both Moses and Elijah served. Their appearance confirms that Lord as the God of life, the one who will raise from the dead all those who remain faithful. Mark's account also reveals God as one who transfigures people and transforms all of us into another mode of being.

> **MARK 9:4** *There appeared . . . Elijah with Moses, who were talking with Jesus.*

Resurrection announced

We look for life in all the wrong people, places, and things. But the fullness of life is not experienced in finding the right relationship, moving to the town with the driest air, or purchasing the latest computer. Jesus taught us that the meaning of life is found on the other side of the grave. We need not be amazed at this, for what we have spent our lives seeking has been stirring within us all along.

> **MARK 16:5-6** *A young man, dressed in a white robe, sitting on the right side [of the tomb] said to [Mary Magdalene, and Mary the mother of James, and Salome], "Do not be alarmed; you are looking for Jesus of Nazareth, who was crucified. He has been raised; he is not here."*

Please pass the potatoes

Every time we eat a meal, we are transformed physically from what we were not into what we are in the process of becoming. Likewise, we are changed spiritually by the others with whom we share the food. They not only pass the potatoes, but they pass themselves around as well. Our hunger for food parallels our hunger for social nourishment. Through the sharing of food, we offer one another support so that we can not only be satisfied but also be raised to new life.

> **LUKE 24:30-31** *When [Jesus] was at the table with them, he took bread, blessed and broke it, and gave it to them. Then their eyes were opened, and they recognized him; and he vanished from their sight.*

Good-bye and hello

❧ We know how hard it is to say good-bye to a member of the family or a close friend pulling up roots and moving to another town or city. We ministers find ourselves saying good-bye quite often, and our congregations must bid us farewell, too. But with every good-bye there is also a hello. Saying good-bye is an act of relinquishing those whom we love and, simultaneously, being relinquished by those who love us. Saying hello is an act of receiving others into our lives and, simultaneously, being received by others into their lives. This prefigures our very process of death and resurrection.

> **JOHN 16:7** *[Jesus said,] "I tell you the truth: it is to your advantage that I go away, for if I do not go away, the Advocate will not come to you; but if go, I will send him to you."*

Drink deeply of the Spirit

❧ We ministers have experienced some strong, driving force in our lives that blew us in the right direction. This force may have been a concerned parent, a teacher, a trusted friend, a business associate, a wise counselor, or ourselves. The push was so potent that it motivated us to change the very course of our lives. We felt as if we were on fire. Incidents abound of those of us who have broken out of our quiet shells and begun to speak with a noisy wisdom that even we did not think possible. We have drunk deeply of resurrected life and are filled with a new Spirit.

ACTS 2:2, 4 *Suddenly from heaven there came a sound like the rush of a violent wind, and it filled the entire house where they were sitting. All of them were filled with the Holy Spirit.*

Sent

The final aspect of ministry is discipleship—being sent to others to spark change in them, even as we are beginning the process all over again for ourselves. Baptism gives us both the responsibility and the authority to make disciples of others, but we know that the best evangelizing tool is the witness of our own lives, which is more effective than any sermon, TV broadcast, or radio spot. When we live as Jesus lived—with the in-breaking of God's reign upon us—we have evangelized as he did.

> **MATTHEW 28:19** *[Jesus said to his disciples,] "Go therefore and make disciples of all nations."*

Other Resources for Ministry

The Catholic Source Book
Rev. Peter Klein

Contains the essential teachings and basic texts of Catholic beliefs, prayers, practices and traditions. It is filled with clear, concise, accurate information on scripture, sacraments, doctrine, the liturgical year, devotions, saints and heroes, councils and popes, church history, religious practices and customs, Catholic symbols, and much more. ISBN: 0-15-950653-0, $18.95

A Contemporary Celtic Prayer Book
William John Fitzgerald

A unique and beautiful hardcover prayer book that captures the flavor and sensibility of traditional Celtic spirituality for today's Christians. The first part of the book contains a simplified Liturgy of the Hours for a seven-day period. The second part is a treasury of Celtic prayers and blessings for a variety of ordinary and special occasions. ISBN: 0-87946-189-6, $16.95

Jesus and His Message
An Introduction to the Good News
Rev. Leo T. Mahon

A clear, concise introduction to who Jesus was and what he taught. Written in an easy-to-understand style, it focuses on Jesus' ministry of teaching and healing, his passion, death and resurrection. The practical, down-to-earth format complete with discussion/reflection questions makes this book perfect for individuals and for use in small faith communities, RCIA programs and adult education classes. ISBN: 0-87946-211-6, $6.95

Protect Us from All Anxiety
Meditations for the Depressed
William Burke, drawings by Mary Southard

A journey from "night" to "dawn" to "day" through fifty powerful reflections on depression and its devastating effects, written by a priest who suffers from depression himself. Each meditation illuminates one aspect of depression and links it with a familiar Bible passage and a heartfelt prayer. "If I were a priest or counselor, I'd have 50 of these books to give to people who suffer from anxiety or depression. The problem is that big and the book is that good," wrote one reviewer. ISBN: 0-87946-184-5, $9.95

Available from booksellers or call 800-397-2282.